RAILWAYS
ROUND
EXMOOR

Robin Madge & Allan Stanistreet

First printed 1971; second edition 1975;
third (revised) edition 1988.
Fourth (revised) edition in 2017

British Library Cataloguing-in-Publication Data
A CIP record for this title is available from the
British Library

ISBN 978 0 85710 110 5

PiXZ Books
Halsgrove House, Ryelands Business Park,
Bagley Road, Wellington, Somerset TA21 9PZ
Tel: 01823 653777
Fax: 01823 216796
email: sales@halsgrove.com

An imprint of Halstar Ltd, part of the
Halsgrove group of companies
Information on all Halsgrove titles is
available at: www.halsgrove.com

Printed and bound by Parksons Graphics, India

Contents

Opposite: *Norton Fitzwarren Junction looking towards the Minehead and Barnstaple branch lines.* (R.J. Sellick Collection)

Title page: *Washford Station.* (Steve Edge)

THE RAILWAYS OF EXMOOR

STANDARD GAUGE

▬▬▬▬	Double, open
▬▬▬▬	Single, open
▬▬▬▬	Single (formerly double), open
———	Double, closed
▬▬▬	Single, closed
———	Other railways, open
--------	Other railways, closed

NARROW GAUGE

+++++	Closed
▬▬▬▬	Open
--------	Projected

STATIONS

◉	Original, open
○	Original, closed
○	Recently opened

0 ——————— 5 miles

Map by @SteveEdgeMaps 2016
Based on open source data from SRTM, OSM & NLS

4

Early morning goods to Taunton with ex. GW pannier tank leaving Bathealton tunnel, 28 May, 1955. (P.T. Waylett)

One of the first trains into Watchet, drawn by a B & ER saddletank, c.1862. (H.H. Hole)

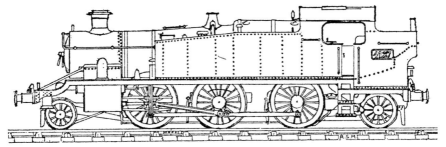

Etching of 4127. GWR Large Prairie.

Introduction to the fourth edition (2017)

It is over forty years since the late Robin Madge, then head of the art department at Huish's Grammar School, Taunton and a railway modeller and enthusiast, first wrote *Railways Round Exmoor*. Much has happened in the intervening years, particularly with regard to the Minehead and Lynton and Barnstaple lines, so it was thought that a new edition describing more recent developments along all the lines originally covered might be timely.

This new edition has been completely re-designed and unlike the original, is now presented in hardback with colour illustrations. The compiler has been at pains to retain as much as possible of Robin's original text, although inevitably a certain amount of editing and amending has been necessary.

The modern visitor to Exmoor could well be surprised that ten railway lines once encircled or pushed up into the terrain now enjoyed principally for its scenic beauty. With three exceptions, all are now extinct; indeed, two never came fully into fruition. Traces of these routes can be recognised by the visitor if he or she is guided in what to look for and is prepared to recognise also that much is now private property. It is also interesting to see the dependence of the various communities in the area on their local branch lines, which still remain in the memory of the older generations.

The earliest line was surprising in that it was an industrial line, built to transport newly found iron ore from the Brendon Hills to the harbour at Watchet and thence by sea to the steelworks of Ebbw Vale. The Taunton-

Minehead and Taunton-Barnstaple lines followed and shortly afterwards the Barnstaple-Ilfracombe line opened. All three were designed both as a means of communication and to encourage tourists to visit the resorts. The Exe Valley Railway completed a useful link between the Devonshire county town of Exeter and the northern part of that county.

Two narrow gauge lines were completed late in the nineteenth century, one again industrial and one with passenger communication in mind. The South Molton-Heasley Mineral Railway was very modest and used horses for propulsion. The Lynton-Barnstaple line was much more ambitious and has become much more widely known in more recent times by some excellent old film footage given national viewing time on television.

The Lynton-Lynmouth Cliff Railway is unique in that it still exists today without a break since its inception in 1890. The remaining two lines were never completed. The Simonsbath-Porlock Weir Railway nearly made it; the track bed was laid ready for the rails and it was designed to take ore from the heart of Exmoor to the harbour at Porlock Weir, much in the manner from the Brendon Hills to Watchet.

The Minehead-Lynmouth route was unashamedly a grandiose scheme to promote tourism but it fell victim to the landed gentry. Some other tentative proposals for lines in or to the area should be listed for historical interest in chronological order, derived from Tuck's *Shareholders' Manual* and other sources.

1845 Somersetshire and North Devon Junction Railway; Bridgwater-Minehead-Porlock.

Bridgwater and Minehead Railway with branches from Williton to Watchet and Washford to Luxborough, laid out for through traffic from Watchet to Luxborough (actually Pool Quay, near Kingsbridge).

Roadwater to Washford; possibly part of the above project and apparently a precursor of the WSMR by about ten years.

The Bristol and English Channels Direct Railway; Watchet-Lyme Regis (Dorset), with branches to Wiveliscombe and Crewkerne.

Exeter, Tiverton, Minehead and Ilfracombe Railway; possibly a steam successor to an 1833 proposal for a "horse railway" from Exeter to Minehead.

1846 The Great Western Extension Atmospheric Railway; Exeter-Barnstaple-Ilfracombe, with branches to Bideford and South Molton. The 'Atmospheric' was a system of propelling trains by creating a vacuum in a pipe between the rails and in so doing drawing the train along. It was tried out in several places. Brunel's experiment between Exeter and Newton Abbot, was the most successful and ran for about eight months but failed in 1848 due to insurmountable mechanical difficulties. In 1847, a rival proposal (not atmospheric) was advanced by the Taw Vale Company, which was controlled by the L. & S.W.R.. Neither scheme was proceeded with and South Molton had to wait for the Taunton-Barnstaple to be served by a station a mile distant.

1877 The Barle Valley Railway (see page 117).

1883 Bridgwater and Watchet Railway; a proposal to link the Somerset and Dorset branch line to Bridgwater with the W.S.R. and W.S.M.R. at Watchet.

1885 The Bray Valley Railway (see page 117).

There is evidence from many of these plans of a desire to make a land crossing of the south-west peninsula, obviating the long sea haul round Land's End but traffic was insufficient to warrant the tremendous expenditure that would have been incurred in building the lines and in the necessary development of the small ports involved.

Because of space constraints, details of events on the two heritage railways have, perforce, been kept as brief as possible, since there are many published works on both lines, particularly the West Somerset Railway.

I am indebted to my friend Steve Edge for his usual highly professional work in drawing the map and to Sharon O'Inn and Steven Pugsley for their assistance and encouragement. Thanks are also due to Alan and Christine Hammond for help with proof reading.

Allan Stanistreet
Watchet, March 2017

Tone Viaduct on 22 June 1963 with the 1755 train from Taunton to Barnstaple. (M.J. Fox)

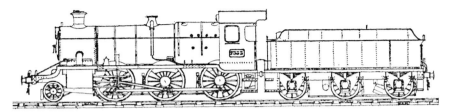

7333. GWR 2-6-0 Mogul. Large cab series.

Taunton – Barnstaple

This was the longest of the lines round Exmoor. Born as the Devon and Somerset Railway, it always had money troubles, which both delayed its early growth and hastened its end, notwithstanding some halcyon summers in the mid-1930s. Even so, the route was so attractive that after the metals had been ripped up and some of the bridges removed, the Exmoor Society promoted an imaginative plan to convert the eastern half, from Norton Fitzwarren to East Anstey, about 22 miles long, into a greenway, as a means of access into and around the National Park for walkers and riders.

History

The earliest plans to link Taunton and Barnstaple with a single track line across the southern approaches to Exmoor were made in the 1840s but it was not until 1873 that the first train ran right through. Yet to the promoters it seemed a logical and simple step to connect the North Devon holiday resorts to the main railway network, extending westwards from Bristol through Taunton. The Act for the 43 miles between Norton Fitzwarren, the junction point on the main line, and Barnstaple was passed in July 1864, after an earlier scheme had been rejected by Parliament some twenty years previously. In the meantime, the 'gauge war' had been the cause of much bickering between the Great Western Railway and its constituent companies on the one hand (favouring the broad gauge of 7ft. ¼in.) and the London and South Western Railway on the other (favouring the standard gauge of 4ft. 8½in.). Indeed, the entry of the L.S.W.R. into Devon and Cornwall was only hindered by lack of capital, following the age of 'railway mania'. In 1864 it had been hoped to extend the broad gauge beyond Barnstaple to connect Ilfracombe to the main

Bristol-Exeter line. This failed, however, since a rival Bill secured the Barnstaple-Ilfracombe section for the opposing interests, which duly opened the line ten years later on 20 July 1874.

The D. & S.R. then set about negotiating with the L.S.W.R. with a view to becoming joint owners of the Ilfracombe line. By 1866, however, financial stringency not only precluded this but made even the continuing construction of the line westwards from Norton Fitzwarren a perilous procedure. Funds fell so low in the summer of 1866 that many of the labouring navvies had to be discharged and some seventy of them marched on Wiveliscombe demanding bread and beer; soon after, in September, cholera struck the impoverished gangs and work came to a standstill. In spite of this, the company was authorised to extend the line in Barnstaple to what would have been a centrally situated terminus in the Square but again, lack of money killed the plan outright. Not until 1870 did fresh finance make possible a resumption of work and the opening, on 8 June 1871, of the 7½ mile section to Wiveliscombe. There was still a 35-mile run to complete; and owing to further constructional difficulties, more than two years were to elapse before the first train ran all the way to Barnstaple. The date was 1 November 1873.

At the celebration lunch at South Molton a week later, the chairman of the company, Lord Poltimore, told the 560 guests that he and his fellow directors had imagined the construction of a railway to be 'an easy task and that the whole thing appeared as if it had only to be undertaken to be finished, but we suddenly fell upon a period of entire and utter confusion in which everything we did at the moment was wrong. Some had been for letting the project die a natural death but he and others had felt honour bound to 'stick to the ship as long as she was above water'. The line, which had cost £21,000 a mile to build, remained broad gauge for only eight years – exactly the same length of time as its sister line from Norton Fitzwarren to Minehead. Both lines were then converted to standard gauge: the Barnstaple line late in 1881, followed by the Minehead line in 1882.

In its early days, the Barnstaple line came in for much criticism, particularly from the Bristol and Exeter Railway, the main line company. The train service was so inconvenient and unreliable that by 1876 it was found imperative to increase the number of crossing loops to six (initially there had been only three) and to make improvements to Barnstaple Station. Later, extra sidings

Dulverton Station before 1890. (L. How Collection)

Dulverton Station 1895. (Dulverton Heritage Centre)

and a further crossing loop were installed at Milverton. David St. John Thomas comments:

'At first the train service was scandalous; mails were not carried because of a disagreement over terms and coal was prohibited from travelling up to Barnstaple. The Bristol and Exeter, which leased the railway, expected to deliver coal imported at Bridgwater to South Molton but the town's merchants boycotted it and for some time continued collecting their stocks by road.'

The B. & E.R. was itself leased to the G.W.R. in 1876. Thanks to this and other changes and to the fact that the Barnstaple line was now being operated by the G.W.R., things began to take a more favourable turn. Moreover, in 1887, a connecting spur was built from the D. & S.R. station at Victoria Road to the L.S.W.R. at Barnstaple Junction. This made possible the profitable through-running of expresses from the Taunton direction and placed Ilfracombe within 225 miles of Paddington via Bristol. However, profits were not sufficient to prevent a take-over by the G.W.R. in 1901, the latter accepting arrears of interest amounting to some £500,000. After that date, as with the Minehead line, operation continued uneventfully until the mid-1930s, when certain developments were authorised: namely, extensions of crossing loops, the doubling of the section between Norton Fitzwarren and Milverton and the introduction of automatic token exchange apparatus of the Whitaker pattern (as used on the neighbouring Somerset and Dorset Railway). When all the main line traffic from London to the west had to go *via* Bristol, the journey from Paddington to Ilfracombe was never less than seven hours but after the G.W.R. had established the shortened route *via* Westbury in 1906, the run was reduced to a record of four hours and fifty-five minutes. After the last war, however, a gradual decline set in. The line steadily lost both its passenger and goods traffic, until, at last, goods ceased in August 1964 and finally, after a short reprieve, the passenger service came to an end on 3 October 1966. The line had lasted ninety-three years.

Route – Taunton to Dulverton

The Barnstaple branch left the main line at Norton Fitzwarren, which also served as the junction for Minehead. In G.W.R. days these two lines were treated as 'twins', since the two services generally left Taunton within five minutes of each other – the Barnstaple train usually ahead of the Minehead. Thus it was a common sight at Norton, shortly after the westwards headlong

Milverton. (Robin Madge)

rush of a main line express, with which the two branches connected, for the Barnstaple train to draw up at the down main platform just before the Minehead train came into the down relief platform. This, of course, was made possible by the fact that all four main roads of the main line were connected to the two branches. It was only in the closing years that the main line connections were taken out; to facilitate speed-up on the main line service, now diesel operated. Before 1934, tokens for both branches were taken at Norton; thereafter, the doubling of the first stages of each line made this time-consuming operation unnecessary.

The route rose on a gradient of 1 in 70 as far as Milverton, where the single line section began and where the first single line token was taken. Then followed a 2-mile ascent to Wiveliscombe, with 1 in 70 and 1 in 60 gradients, offering frequent glimpses of the southern slopes of the Brendon Hills, with the Exmoor heights beyond. It was here that an incident took place, as related by the fireman concerned.

Whereas passenger trains were able to exchange tokens in a leisurely fashion during the halt at Wiveliscombe, goods trains heading west preferred to pick up the token at a smart pace. Immediately ahead lay a section steepening to 1 in 58 for nearly 2 miles into Bathealton Tunnel. This was no place to linger owing to the restricted clearance and because fumes from the locomotive, aggravated by the engine being worked flat out, were particularly obnoxious: indeed, many tales were told of the handrails of tenders bearing a coat of yellow sulphur by the time the train had reached the far end of this quarter-mile long tunnel. On this particular day, a passenger train to Taunton was waiting safely in the up side of the station at Wiveliscombe, so that the token would be readily available to the goods train. Regulations demanded that a train be slowed to 10 miles an hour to effect a hand-change (Whitaker's apparatus was not fitted to all engines). However, the fireman of the goods train had developed the art of catching the token smartly on the coal pick at speeds of up to 40 miles an hour (highly illegal). The token to be dropped was skidded along the platform and, if luck and judgement were in favour, it often came to rest within a few feet of the duty signalman. Accordingly, the exchange was accomplished at a spanking pace, the hill attacked in fine style, the tunnel safely negotiated, so that eventually the train reached Venn Cross without a check. But on this occasion the crew were met by the signalman at Venn enquiring after the token that should have been dropped

Dulverton Station 1928. (Dulverton Heritage Centre)

Dulverton Station goods yard showing the old and new cranes, 1928.
(Dulverton Heritage Centre)

Lorry driver Jack Vellacott at Dulverton Station, 1928.
(Dulverton Heritage Centre)

Dulverton Station, c.1900. (Dulverton Heritage Centre)

at Wiveliscombe. Where was it? The passenger train was still waiting there and could not proceed to Taunton without it. Alas, the token was not found that day, nor the next and it was not until some six months later that it turned up on the track at Snow Hill Station, Birmingham. What had happened was that the token had bounced off the platform at Wiveliscombe, passed through the moving goods train and lodged in the under-framing of one of the passenger coaches, only to drop off some months later in 'foreign territory'!

Between the long tunnel (445 yards) at Bathealton and the shorter one (246 yards) just before Venn Cross, the line crossed the most prominent architectural feature of the whole route: the Waterrow Viaduct, a lattice girder structure, 162 yards long, by which the line crossed the River Tone. Latterly, the viaduct caused concern, owing to the need for renovation and reinforcement, undoubtedly a strong factor behind the decision to close the line. Nonetheless, it was a fine example of Victorian engineering. At Venn Cross the railway both entered Devon and reached the second highest point of the route (666 feet), where snow would often block the track due to drifting in the cutting. Falling gradients then took the line due west for some 3½ miles to Morebath Station (2 miles from the village), and for a further 1½ miles to Morebath Junction Halt, where the Exe Valley branch came up from Bampton.

The halt, a mere half-mile from Morebath, was very poorly served in terms of platform accommodation or shelter, yet it boasted a passing loop for the convenience of train operation.

Two accidents

Signalman Frank Challis was thirty-five years in the box at Morebath before his retirement to Bampton in 1960. One of his most treasured memories was of the morning of 4 November 1940, when he signalled the Plymouth express – or what was left of it – through his section. In the early hours the train had been derailed at Norton Fitzwarren with heavy loss of life and, with the main west of England line blocked, it was re-routed *via* Dulverton, back to Morebath junction and then down the Exe Valley to Exeter.

Frank learned later that the 9.40 p.m. sleeping-car express from Paddington, drawn by 'King' class 4-6-0 locomotive *King George VI*, had been delayed by air raids and was an hour late at Taunton. There it had been diverted to the relief line to let through a fast newspaper train. The driver, from Paddington, wearied by delays and the strain of wartime conditions (his own house had been bombed shortly before he came on duty) forgot that he was on the relief line and took the newspaper train's signals for his own. Realising his mistake too late, he applied the brakes but went through the trap-points at the end of the relief line. Twenty-seven people, including the fireman, were killed and 75 injured. Just how near the newspaper train came to disaster as well can be gauged by the fact that, as it passed the express, the guard heard his window smash and a bolt landed at his feet. This, it transpired later, had been flung from the buffer beam of the wrecked locomotive at the moment of impact.

Just fifty years earlier, on 11 November 1890, a slow goods train had been shunted on to the up line at Norton Fitzwarren to allow a fast down goods to pass. It was a dark night and after the fast train had gone through, the signalman overlooked the slow goods on the up line and signalled the right-of-way to a London-bound passenger train. It tore through the station at high speed, following its passage down Wellington bank and crashed into the goods train, killing ten people.

These tragic occurrences in the same vicinity were, in fact, among the very few major accidents to happen over the whole of the G.W.R network for a period of more than half-a-century.

Dulverton to Barnstaple

Three-quarters of a mile west of Morebath Junction, the line re-entered Somerset by a bridge over the River Exe, just south of its confluence with the River Barle and crossed the charming valley on the flank of Dulverton Station. Here is another misnomer, for the station was at Brushford, a distinct and thriving village 2 miles south of Dulverton proper. The station was quite imposing by branch line standards. It had only a longish up platform with appropriate buildings but the down platform was an island, the outside face acting as the terminus of the Exe Valley line and signalled accordingly. Goods sidings, generously spaced, completed the lay-out, which even included a locomotive turntable. In its heyday the station was a busy one, with visitors who stayed at the Carnarvon Arms and the Dulverton hotels for fishing and hunting; a bus to meet all the trains, clanking milk churns for the dairy farms, horse and cattle trucks at the loading bay, coal heaps on one side of the yard and on the other, on one occasion, an entire train load of sugar beet pulp all the way from East Anglia. It achieved distinction, too, when, late in the last war, General Eisenhower arrived in his personal train to visit American troops stationed on Exmoor. The G.W.R. put several carriages of the 'special saloon' class at his disposal.

West of Dulverton the line entered a delightful stretch of 'forgotten' country; an intimate jungle of overgrown copses, hedges and banks running straight up and down hills, bogs and streams in the bottoms. By day, an observant passenger would spy a farm by its roof half-hidden in the trees, by night he might spot a farmer with a lamp on his rounds. The going was hard: a 4-mile stretch of severe gradients, including one of 1 in 58, before reaching East Anstey, the summit of the line (c.700ft.). After that, the running was easier, downhill past Yeo Mill Halt (opened in 1932) and due west to Bishop's Nympton and Molland Station, both villages being roughly equidistant, 2-3 miles away. The line then followed on over two small but sporting fishing rivers, the Yeo and the Mole, before reaching South Molton Station, three-quarters of a mile north of the town and, before the days of myxomatosis, renowned for the 'rabbit special' that carried a regular load to up-country markets.

The line passed through gentler country for the remainder of the route to Barnstaple, though the section through the Fortescue estate, at Castle Hill, had several remarkable features: first, Bremridge Tunnel (321 yards); then Filleigh Viaduct, a six-span lattice girder bridge 232 yards long over the river

The very realistic model of Dulverton Station, as it appeared in the inter-war period, at the Dulverton Heritage Centre. (Andrew Williams)

Bray; and some entrancing views. Filleigh was originally called Castle Hill but it was changed in 1881 to avoid confusion with a London suburban station of the same name, now, however, familiar as West Ealing. Swimbridge was the last intermediate station on the branch and after passing the linking line to the Southern Railway at Barnstaple Junction, you arrived at the G.W.R. terminus. The 43-mile journey from Taunton averaged one-and-three-quarter hours.

Engines and rolling stock

The operation of this line has never been recorded in any great detail in the technical press and the columns of *The Railway Magazine* are the best source for research. A full account by H.A. Vallance in the issue of June 1957 states that 'after 1881 various types of 2-4-0, 4-4-0 and 0-6-0 tender locomotives were used'. It is certain, however, that after about 1925, the bulk of the traffic was handled by G.W.R. 2-6-0 'Mogul' tender engines, these being preferred to the

The last steam train at East Anstey Station before Dr Beeching closed the Taunton-Barnstaple line. (Michael Deering)

Dulverton Station on 22 June 1963 with loco 6372 on the 16.22 train leaving for Barnstaple, and loco 1421 on an Exeter train in the bay. (M.J. Fox)

tank versions, probably due to heavier coal and water carrying capacities of the former – an insurance on the long journey westwards from Taunton. Diesel multiple units operated the line towards the end.

The coaches were almost always corridor stock and the usual make-up was of three or four coaches, augmented at times of heavy traffic to a maximum of nine. A horse box was often towed at the rear. Owing to the link with the S.R. at Barnstaple, it was by no means uncommon to see S.R. green coaches on Barnstaple trains working into Taunton. This made it possible to see all

Dulverton, mid-1960s, as the signalman exchanges the token with the second man of a diverted West of England express, headed by an unidentified 'Warship'. (Chris Jones)

four main line companies together at times in Taunton Station: L.M.S. 'crimson lake' on the Liverpool and Manchester trains and on the 'Devonian' from Bradford, while L.N.E.R. 'teak' regularly appeared on the through workings between Cornwall and Newcastle.

Epilogue

For those who lived along the line, the Taunton-Barnstaple branch was an object of affection. The trains were generally punctual and men working in the fields near, say, Brushford, could safely rely on the 5.00 p.m. train to Taunton to tell them when to knock off work. It was no trouble to send or receive parcels and the guard was always willing to post a late letter on Taunton Station. The railway had other, incidental, uses. For example, to train a young horse for traffic, a farmer would turn it into a field beside the track, where familiarity with the snorting monsters soon gave it confidence on the road. After nationalisation, the staff steadily lost heart and what once had been regulations guided by common sense became regulations for their own sake. Farmers, for instance, could no longer bargain for return trucks after market; they had to pay the full rate or none and so the long-distance cattle trade was hastened into the hands of the road hauliers. Even the undoubted value of the line during the great freeze of 1962-3 made no permanent impression. Many people sledged to the stations to collect supplies brought by the trains and at Dulverton Station helicopters landed to load provisions for the farms and hamlets cut off on the high moor. The line became a lifeline but when spring came, good weather dissolved all the earlier resolutions. The line was already doomed.

Postscript

Most of the line has been absorbed into the landscape, though some of the infrastructure survives. Some parts , for example at Milverton, have been used to improve the local roads. A number of the station houses and goods sheds have been adapted for dwellings and other uses. The piers of Waterrow viaduct remained to be seen many years after closure. Perhaps most notably, a short length of the track bed at Norton Fitzwarren, as far as the remains of Allerford Bridge, has been reclaimed by the West Somerset Railway as part of its turning triangle and this stretch is used for brake van rides during the West Somerset Railway Association's Steam Fayre and Vintage Vehicle Rally held on the first weekend of August.

Dulverton Station in the 1970s. (Dulverton Heritage Centre)

Dulverton Station today.

The Taunton-Barnstaple viaduct at Filleigh which now carries the North Devon Link Road.

Leighwood Auto, 9 Oct 2016. (Steve Edge)

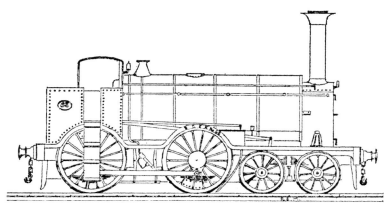

No. 68. B & E 4-4-0 Saddle tank.

Taunton – Minehead

This line was the product of two separate enterprises, whose prime purpose was to provide additional outlets for the iron ore traffic from the Brendon Hills.

History

In November 1856, plans were deposited by the West Somerset Railway for a broad gauge line from Norton Fitzwarren (on the Bristol and Exeter Railway) to Watchet, a distance of 14½ miles. Nominally, Isambard Kingdom Brunel was the engineer in charge, though it is fairly certain that his deputy, R.P. Brereton, did most of the work. The second stage was to run an extension from the present station at Watchet (as the terminus of the line) to the West Somerset Mineral Railway at Whitehall and, since the latter line used the standard gauge, to convert the track to mixed. The W.S.M.R. objected, however, and so this part of the plan (though in essence the prime purpose of the railway) was not included in the W.S.R. Act of 1857. Owing to bad weather and other difficulties, construction proceeded slowly and it was not until 31 March 1862 that the line, including an extension to Watchet east pier, was officially opened to traffic.

The construction of the 8¼-mile route from Watchet to Minehead was competed for but had to wait twelve years for completion. The first plan had been laid by the W.S.M.R. in 1856, when Henry Fownes Luttrell, of Dunster Castle, offered free access to Minehead harbour; but though prepared by Rice Hopkins, engineer of the W.S.M.R., it never materialised. A second plan, this time for a broad gauge line to be built by a local company, the Minehead Railway, was authorised in 1865, the engineer being R.P. Brereton. In this case, the main difficulty was the section between Watchet and Washford, where, following opposition by the W.S.M.R. to a mixed gauge, the two tracks, one broad and one standard eventually ran alongside one another. However, for financial reasons this plan had to be shelved too. A third attempt, after the company had been reconstituted in 1871, finally found success. Brereton's plans were adopted and despite customary troubles over labour and terrain, the extension to Minehead, continued from a so-called 'end-to-end' junction at Watchet, was finally opened on 16 July 1874. Thus, the 24¾-mile through route from Taunton was at last complete. It ran, however, for only eight years in broad gauge before conversion to standard in October 1882, the whole length being completed in one day, though full services were not restored for a further day or two.

The line operated uneventfully until the early 1930s, when, as part of a policy of development throughout the G.W.R. system, to help offset national unemployment, two new crossing loops were constructed at Kentsford Farm, between Watchet and Washford, and Leigh Wood, between Crowcombe and Stogumber, automatic token exchange apparatus installed and the track doubled from Dunster to Minehead, as later from Norton Fitzwarren to Bishops Lydeard. These sections were operated as single track a few years before the end of the line under British Railways in January 1971.

Route – Taunton to Watchet

The junction at Norton Fitzwarren was the starting point of this, as of the Barnstaple line. Moreover, sited as it was at the end of a four-track section from Cogload, junction of the Bristol and Westbury lines east of Taunton, the Norton signal box was an important one and carried one of the longest name boards on the system. It is now displayed in the Gauge Museum at Bishops Lydeard. Access to and from the Minehead branch was either from the main or relief roads until latterly, when the main lines were entirely segregated. After the track to Bishops Lydeard had been singled, the Norton box was closed.

Floods at Williton Station in December 1929. (H.H. Hole)

Four-coupled GWR tank heads a train of 4- and 6-wheelers out of Watchet towards Minehead. (A.L. Wedlake Collection)

The 'Quantock Belle' crossing Woolston Moor, May 1984. (Stephen Edge)

From Norton, the line curved away northward on a gradient of 1 in 85 to Bishops Lydeard, a pleasant little country station with modest buildings on the down side and a corrugated iron shelter on the up platform. The station master's house, quite an imposing structure, was separated from the down platform by a siding into the goods shed. Thereafter, the line ran single to Crowcombe, rising on a gradient of 1in 80, through charming countryside, backed by the Brendons to the west and the Quantocks to the east. You could generally see a heron standing sentinel by the brook beside the grounds of Connaught House. In spring, the cuttings between Combe Florey and Crowcombe were massed with primroses, to a degree only equalled by those on the banks between Crowcombe and Stogumber; a display as worthy of the title of 'The Primrose Line' as the 'Bluebell Line' is in Sussex. Here the gradient often troubled locomotives on the Minehead run and a train would stop to allow sufficient steam to be raised before creeping into Crowcombe; yet another instance of the way the G.W.R. would build its stations at some distance from the villages they were supposed to serve.

Here was a passing loop and a single siding used to load stone from the nearby Triscombe quarry in the Quantocks. Crowcombe (since renamed Crowcombe Heathfield as it was originally) remains a delightful place in the summer but winter could be a very different story. There are memories of snow-covered rails and of a day in 1963 when the whole station was so blanketed by a blizzard that not a train ran. Another evening, in February 1965, (the line was being worked by 3-car diesel sets then) when a sudden snowstorm enveloped the district and the last train from Taunton at 8.45 p.m. had been held for some forty minutes to ensure a connection with the 5.30 p.m. from Paddington, itself delayed by snow further up the line. The last train from Minehead actually pulled in before the Taunton train left at about 9.30 p.m. A further wait took place at Norton, while the points were cleared of snow and then it trundled on to Crowcombe, arriving at about 9.50 p.m. There it stayed and it was duly learned that the telegraph to Williton had failed and rendered the token exchange inoperable. Imagine the frustration when it was realised that nobody was willing to allow the train forward and passengers were compelled to sit under a curtain of falling snow until 11.30 p.m. Ultimately, a police car arrived with a pilot man, who took the train on but the train didn't reach Minehead before midnight, some two-and-three-quarter-hours late. Summer delights seemed very far away then. Crowcombe, and other parts of the line, also featured on film, in some of the sequences of *The Belstone Fox* and the Beatles' *A Hard Day's Night*. The absence rate in the local schools rose alarmingly when the latter's film company was at work!

After Crowcombe, the line dropped away sharply at 1 in 68 to Stogumber, passing the Leigh loop *en route*. This was only used on Saturdays in normal service, to facilitate the passage of holiday excursions to Minehead and the signal box was switched in and out as required. Nearby was the level crossing at Leigh Woods, controlled by a crossing keeper, as was the one at Roebuck. Rumour had it that more than one train made an unscheduled halt at the lonely bungalow while the engine crew enjoyed unscheduled refreshments in return for goods delivered.

As elsewhere, Stogumber and its station were at least a mile apart, the latter consisting of a wooden platform with a plain shelter, a single siding to a goods shed and a spur for a camping coach. On one side the line had been cut into the hill, the ground falling away from the platform to a point about 100 feet below rail level, so that the station seemed to have been built on a shelf; a striking example of the disproportionate effort and expense so often incurred when constructing these small branch lines. It is hard now to appreciate the revolutionary role played by railways in opening up the countryside and to understand the high hopes that people placed upon their future.

At Williton all was laid out on an imposing scale; even the 'six foot', that is, the gap between the tracks, was abnormal due to the station having been laid out to broad gauge specifications (the only one on the branch). A water tower furnished ample refreshment to the engines on completion of the hill section from Crowcombe, or before they attempted it, and there was an extensive goods yard. There was an occasion in the early 1960s when, after a night of exceptional rain, the morning train from Minehead had to be replaced by a bus, put on at short notice to collect intending passengers from the intermediate stations and take them as far as Crowcombe, where the real train was waiting for its daily load of regulars. All had gone well up to Watchet but on approaching Williton Station, it was seen that what had been a double track was now a raging river, muddy water running level with the tops of the platforms. Stogumber was in similar case but fortunately the floods subsided as quickly as they had risen and later in the day normal working was resumed.

'Fruit ripe, ripe fruit'. This was the cry heard regularly at Williton, at least until 1935/6, when Harold and Charles Martin, father and son, of the local firm of J. Jones and Son, florists and nurserymen, exercised their right to go on to the platform with a fruit basket and sell to passengers. The concession had probably first been granted when the railway reached Williton in 1862. It was revived for one day, the last day of the line, on 2 January 1971, by Edward Martin, Charles' ten-year-old son.

The line from Williton ran over flat fields before rounding a curve to meet the sea some 20 feet above high water level. It then proceeded parallel to the shore for about half a mile until it entered a cutting leading into Watchet Station. This stretch had always been a source of anxiety to the railway company owing to coastal erosion and the closure of the line must have saved further heavy expenditure on reinforcement, since in places the distance between the line and the eroded bank had narrowed to about 15 yards.

Watchet

The station was not imposing, merely a single platform and an unpretentious building tucked into the bank. At one time, a complex of goods sidings served the adjoining harbour and the whole layout was further complicated by a pedestrian crossing controlled only by a warning bell, rung when main line trains were due. Trains from either direction signalled their approach by whistling. G.W.R. steam engines carried two whistles; one ostensibly for general warning, the other reserved for shunters and signalmen, each whistle being of a different musical pitch. One driver used to herald his approach by sounding both whistles alternately and so earned himself the nickname of 'The Cuckoo Driver'. He made it all the more realistic by 'cuckooing' late in the evening or early in the morning. During shunting, the inconvenience both to the railway staff and to other people crossing the lines was mutual.

Railway sidings at Watchet Harbour. The stones in front of the GWR 'Iron Mink' van originated as ballast in ships from Ireland, some of them used to face houses in Watchet.
(A.L. Wedlake Collection)

The harbour sidings were used entirely for the traffic in wood pulp, imported from the Scandinavian countries and forwarded a mere half mile to the local paper mill siding. Likewise, in esparto grass from North Africa, shipped into Watchet *en route* for the sister paper mill at Silverton, near Exeter. When a grass boat was in, the harbour was busy all day. A train of open wagons had to be marshalled and, after loading, securely sheeted down before dispatch late in the afternoon. The railway always contended that, owing to the bulk and lightness of the grass, this trade never paid. Suffice it to say that in 1964/5, the grass was transferred to road transport and the sidings removed. This gave Watchet Urban District Council, formed in 1902 to manage the harbour, the chance to buy the surplus land and offer it, on lease, to the shipping companies, which thereupon developed the port with warehouse accommodation. As a result, there was a strong revival of trade, mainly in Baltic timber and in general cargoes from Spain and Portugal. This produced the anomaly of fresh business from which the railway could not benefit, since it depended on the very land that it had already sold. The harbour ceased to trade commercially in January 1993 and it was then converted into a marina.

Watchet and Williton people were probably responsible for one of the 'named' trains of the G.W.R., although the name never appeared in the company's timetables. Before the last war, the Saturday evening train to Taunton offered a cheap return trip, an opportunity seized by many to go into town to buy up at bargain prices the remaining cuts of bacon in the market, for Taunton was renowned for pig meat. So the train came to be known, informally, as 'The Bacon Special'.

Watchet to Minehead

Coming out of Watchet the railway is crossed by a bridge linking the old town with more recent building; a bad bottleneck for road traffic and not expected to survive the closure of the line for very long. It is still there, unchanged, and suffers occasional damage from passing road traffic. Next came two sharp curves, the sharpest on the line, separated by the siding to the paper mill, which was taken out in 1967. At this point, a short uphill gradient often caused difficulty to goods trains, which had stopped to shunt. Frequently, they would fail at first try, had then to run back into Watchet Station and return for another 'stab' at the bank. Next came the section where the line ran parallel to the W.S.M.R. and was used for the trials of the Angus Automatic

Broad gauge days at Minehead. Note the engine shed far left, newly transferred from Watchet, and the B&E tank engine at the station platform. (James Date)

Braking System in July 1912, described on page 108. Here, too, the Kentsford loop was long kept in daily service, serving as the terminus of the numerous troop trains for the army camp at Doniford. Ten and twelve coach sets would pull up, whereupon the two big 41XX tank engines, double-headed, would run round the train to take it back to Taunton.

The best thing about Washford Station was the name board, of an attractive B. & E.R. pattern with seriffed letters, in contrast to the plain block capitals of the G.W.R. Here the line made a detour inland, behind the high cliffs between Watchet and Blue Anchor, only to sweep back again to the coast past Old Cleeve and Cleeve Park, before reaching Dunster and the last straight stretch, in double track, over the marshes to Minehead. At Dunster, the station is ten minutes' walk from the 'picture' village, with its yarn market and castle at either end of the main street, thronged with tourists, very few of whom ever used the railway for their outing. At Minehead, the terminus buildings and station layout, though radically altered in 1934, remained modest and Victorian: an appropriate threshold to the fine natural setting of the town, with North Hill its bastion in the background.

Engines and rolling stock

It is obvious from contemporary photographs that the portly B. & E.R. saddle-tanks of James Pearson were the principal locomotives in the early days, succeeded by the products of Armstrong and Dean, with all their brass and copper embellishments. Remarkably few named engines served the branch, however, despite the popularity of the practice on the G.W.R. It is known that some of the later Bulldog 4-4-0s of the 'Bird' class were stationed at Taunton; while 'Seagull' and 'Chaffinch' were undoubtedly used. Most of the donkey work was done by the various types of pannier tank 0-6-0s which earned themselves the local nickname of 'Matchboxes'. The 45XX and 55XX 2-6-2s were frequently on duty; and one interesting working was of a Yeovil-based 45XX which, for a while, was timetabled on a through run to Minehead and back with its accompanying 'B' set of coaches, (a rake of two similar coach units permanently close-coupled). The 22XX 0-6-0s were often rostered, too, and at least one ran with an ex-Great Central Railway tender, which it had somehow acquired from one of the R.O.D. 2-8-0 engines bought by the G.W.R. after the First World War. They always seemed to make heavy weather of the line and their appearance on the 4.25 p.m. train from Taunton would be greeted with gloom by the regular travellers, as it generally meant getting home late from work. On good days, however, one of the large 2-6-2 tanks of the 41XX or 61XX classes would guarantee a swift passage up the hill to Crowcombe and punctual running all through.

These fine tanks did yeoman service on the Minehead line and always seemed complete masters of their job. The tender equivalents of these engines were equally effective, being equal in every dimension that mattered but they were out of favour with their crews since the turntable at Minehead was too short and could only be used by attaching two extension rails to support the tender wheels. This completely unbalanced the load, so that pushing the engine round became a heavy chore.

Probably the last occasion when this turntable was used was when the ex-L.M.S. engine *Duchess of Hamilton*, a huge 4-6-2 express locomotive, was delivered to Butlin's holiday camp at Minehead. It was pulled dead down the entire line with motion and coupling rods removed, to allow the long wheelbase to negotiate the sharp curves. These were checked afterwards to see if any straightening had occurred before being pushed on to the turntable for transfer to a low-loading lorry and delivery to the camp. Incidentally, due

Minehead Station before reopening. Summer 1974. (Allan Stanistreet)

Volunteers weeding at Watchet prior to reopening, 1974. (Allan Stanistreet)

to a name-swap, this locomotive was sent to America as *Coronation* in 1938 and caught there when war broke out. Not until after the war did she return to Britain and regain her rightful name and number.

The Minehead branch was always remarkable for the variety of rolling stock, right from the early days, when it was G.W.R. practice to label coaches with the time and destination of the train, down to the last days of steam, when many relegated express coaches were used. Thus, after the last war, many of the 9ft. 7 ins. wide centenary coaches ended their days on the branch; luxurious travel indeed. Similarly, the 1947 Hawksworth conversions to slip-coaches made their appearance with the running down of the slip coach services on the main lines. Towards the end, the branch was normally worked with 3-car diesel sets of different patterns, occasionally augmented to 6-cars. On Saturdays in the summer, Inter-City formations found their way on to the branch, in various combinations of 3- and 4-car sets. But the principal excursion trains were of main line stock of B.R. pattern, hauled at first by the D6300 diesels and later by the big D7000 Hymeks; a very handsome design with fibreglass cabs.

The end?

By the late 1960s lessening revenues made it inevitable that the line's contin-uing operation was doomed, despite the fact that stringent economies were made. Thus, there were only eleven staff employed on the branch at closure. Creative accounting probably played a part as well, for the line was still quite busy in the summer months. The date for closure was finally set for 2 January 1971, prior to which all items of value to railway enthusiasts had been removed to safety. The usual obsequies were observed and the line became dormant, although none of it was lifted and it still remained possible, in theory, to travel from Taunton to Minehead by train.

Revival

Even before closure, plans were being made to reopen the line with the intention of running diesel commuter trains, supplemented in the summer by steam trains along a part of the line to attract tourists. The intention was to form a private company to achieve this aim. Much water has flowed under the bridge since then and the railway's revival has not been without its vicis-situdes. In April 1971, a mere three months after closure, a public meeting was held in Taunton to discuss the possibilities of reopening the line as a

Open all hours! Minehead yard, 1976. This sort of thing is no longer permitted.
(Allan Stanistreet)

Volunteers working on the permanent way prior to reopening, 1975.
This is at the top of Washford Bank. (Allan Stanistreet)

Volunteers removing the siding point from Blue Anchor for use at Minehead.
Summer 1975. (Allan Stanistreet)

Bishops Lydeard, 1975. (Allan Stanistreet)

Stogumber sleeps, 1975. (Allan Stanistreet)

Volunteers reinstating the goods shed road at Minehead under the direction of Harold Blackmore (extreme left). (Allan Stanistreet)

Reopening day at Minehead. Not a hi-vis vest in sight! 28 March, 1976. (Allan Stanistreet)

Re-opening Day at Minehead Station on Sunday, 28 March, 1976. (Arthur Phillips)

private enterprise and a working party was formed to investigate the *pros* and *cons*, including the financial implications of reopening. Following their report, a meeting was held in Taunton in May under the chairmanship of Douglas Fear, a Taunton businessman, with a view to forming the West Somerset Private Railway Company (the "Private" was soon dropped). The same month, the West Somerset Railway Association was formed with the aim of supporting the company, with both physical and financial assistance. Despite the optimism that the new organisation would be up and running in short order, it was to be another five years before trains carrying fare-paying passengers were to run. In the meantime, efforts were being made to assemble locomotives and rolling stock to form the trains. Two industrial 0-6-0 saddle tank engines were purchased from Austin at Longbridge: *Victor* and *Vulcan*, two Bagnalls originally built for shunting in the steel works at Margam in South Wales. Two 2-car Park Royal diesel mechanical railcars were also acquired. All this stock was stored in the old Taunton west yard, along with some stock belonging to the Great Western Society.

Inevitably, bureaucracy was to enter the fray, which was to result in many delays before permission was given for the volunteers (the company had no staff until reopening) to begin to tackle the years of dereliction. In the meantime, there were the usual hurdles of private enquiries, objections from residents (and others) and a good deal of obstruction by the National Union of Railwaymen, whose bus-driver members had transferred from the railway when the line closed and were determined that their new occupation would not suffer from competition from any reopened line. This problem was to simmer on for years.

It would take more than this book to write the story of the present W.S.R. Suffice it to say that at least twenty books have been produced about the line since reopening and some of the more relevant will be found in the bibliography.

After reopening, on 28 March 1976, the company suffered almost ten years of an extremely precarious existence, mainly due to poor management, and it is now accepted as an undisputed fact that without the injection of considerable sums by the supporting Association (not then a charity), the line would undoubtedly have gone to the wall. By the mid-1980s, a grip had been taken of the situation and the line finally began to achieve the potential which can be seen today.

Much of what has been achieved is down to the efforts of the volunteer staff, without whose generous provision of time and money the railway simply would not run. The present public limited company employs around 50 paid staff but the bulk of the support comes from 800-1000 volunteers, who come from every walk of life. In more recent years, a lot of the jobs formerly done by manual labour are now done by mechanical means and contractors are engaged for the larger projects.

Notable improvements to the basic railway over the years include the restoration and re-signalling of the crossing loop at Crowcombe Heathfield, the revised layout and re-signalling at Minehead, the development of the works at Williton, together with the recent restoration of the crossing loop to near its original length and many new works at Bishops Lydeard to cope with the increased train services and the fact that it is from this station that most of the passengers start their visit. All this has cost considerable sums of money and the task is ongoing. The infrastructure, already over a century old when the new company took over, requires constant vigilance and attention. For example, there are over 40 miles of fencing to be maintained.

By far the largest projects in recent years have been the refurbishment and installation of the turntable at Minehead, one of the few on a heritage railway, and the planning and construction of the triangle at Norton Fitzwarren. The turntable was acquired from Pwllheli in North Wales in 1977, together with a water tower. Originally a 55-foot table, it languished for many years around Minehead yard in various locations, awaiting the time and money for its

Unloading stone for road improvements at Leigh Lane. Loco 66027.
(Martin Southwood)

installation. Too short for the larger locomotives which might haul charter trains, it was decided to increase its length to 65 feet. This was eventually done and on 11 February 2008, the finished product was finally lowered into place near to the site of the original turntable, watched by a considerable crowd of fascinated onlookers. It is now in regular use and the W.S.R is the only heritage line where it is possible to turn a steam (or diesel) locomotive at

Somerset and Dorset Railway 2-8-0 No.88 (now 53808) on the turntable at Minehead. March 2009. (Steve Edge)

66622 leads The High Output Ballast Cleaner at Norton Fitzwarren on 28 May 2011. Conductor Driver Len Renwick looks out of the cab. (Steve Edge)

each end of its journey. It is also used to turn rolling stock in order to even out wear on wheel flanges. It sees most use on Gala Weekends.

The triangle was first conceived as a project by the Association, led by its then chairman, the late David Holmes. Thirty-three acres of land were purchased for this purpose at Norton Fitzwarren, adjacent to the West of England main line and incorporating the first section of the old Barnstaple branch, with the object of being able to turn trains both on the W.S.R. and outside operators running steam charters on to the line. This required a good deal of planning and civil engineering, as the land lies on a flood plain and much work was required on culverts and land drainage, not to mention many hundreds of yards of (expensive) fencing.

A subsequent bonus was the use of part of the land to dump spent ballast from various relaying projects on Network Rail. The triangle is used regularly for the turning of these trains for their return to Fairwater yard ready for their next duty. This operation still, at the time of writing (2017), brings in much useful revenue to the Association's coffers. The facility is provided in conjunction with the plc.

The early timetables were compiled on a rather *ad hoc* basis, with no proper research as to public demand. In more recent years, a more scientific approach has been adopted and the timetables are now adjusted yearly to reflect the demand. An early experiment also was to have different fares for steam-hauled trains and those of the diesel multiple units (DMU). This turned into something of a nightmare for the Travelling Ticket Inspectors (TTI), who were required to commit the different fares to memory and the experiment was swiftly abandoned!

Trains now run on 244 days a year and included in this total are several Gala Weekends, which see 'guest' locomotives brought in to add interest and these occasions are usually themed. Efforts to encourage future volunteers see certain weekends devoted to children's characters such as Thomas the Tank Engine, Peppa Pig, Fireman Sam and Postman Pat. The West Somerset Railway Association owns the "Quantock Belle", a prestigious dining train, which provides luxury dining for up to 73 people on about twenty days a year, beginning in April and continuing until October. Most of these trains, fully staffed by volunteers, run at lunch time on Sundays but there are

Class 47 47798 **Prince William** *heading the royal train on 1 November 2002. Signalman Martin Southwood exchanges tickets with driver conductor Trevor Barnett. HRH The Duke of Edinburgh was visiting Lynmouth on the fiftieth anniversary of the flood disaster.*
(Martin Southwood)

The steam railmotor at Doniford Halt. (Steve Edge)

Class 59 approaches Blue Anchor from Minehead with stone empties. December 2010.
(Lee Robbins)

The old and the new. GWR 4-6-0 Earl Bathurst *waits to cross with a Virgin Voyager at Blue Anchor.* (Steve Edge)

some Saturday evening trains. Special trains are run during the Christmas period; especially popular is the one which runs in conjunction with the annual "Dunster by Candlelight" event.

Since the railway year begins with February half-term and ends the week after Christmas, a good deal of planning and effort has to go into maintaining the infrastructure and carrying out repairs and maintenance on locomotives and rolling stock. Currently, four timetables are run, depending on the time of year: red with four trains a day each way at the beginning and end of the season; green with five trains each way on the shoulders of the season; orange at the beginning and end of the high season and yellow in high season; usually late July to early September. Red and orange timetable trains are all steam-hauled, while the green and yellow ones have a combination of steam and diesel haulage. Around 200,000 passengers a year are carried.

For some years, the West Somerset Railway has provided a training facility for the main line companies and it may be assumed that the trainees, and their instructors, relish the opportunity to enter such a time capsule. The sheer length of the line gives them plenty of opportunities for seeing how railways were operated for well over a century and of course, the exercise brings in welcome revenue for the company. The line has also been used commercially when trains from the main line companies have brought in stone for various sea defence works over the years. These workings have saved many thousands of lorry journeys over unsuitable local roads.

Signalling is by the traditional G.W.R. lower quadrant semaphore, although all distant signals are fixed. Certain concessions have had to be made to comply with modern legislation and some signals and points are electrically operated, while signal lamps are now all electrically lit. Signalmen (they are still signalmen on the W.S.R.) no longer have to climb signal posts in force 8 gales!

While the purists may complain about all this modernity, there is nothing new about it. The G.W.R. had electrically operated points and colour-light signals before the last war and the signalmen, particularly at Williton, no longer have to have muscles like the world's strongest man to get the points over in that location!

Train running for many years after reopening was regulated by the staff and ticket system. This is simple and basic but is very inflexible. On a single line railway, only one engine (or two coupled together) or train, even when double-headed, may occupy a section at any one time. The reason for this is obvious, as one cannot have two colliding in mid-section. Consequently, the driver of the train engine (never the pilot engine) is given a staff shaped and coloured in a different way for each section, as his authority to proceed. He cannot do so without this. If a second train is to go in the same direction, the driver is shown the staff and given a ticket by the signalman as his authority to proceed. When trains are to move alternately, the staff will be given to the returning train.

With an ever-increasing timetable and more trains running, it became essential to install a more flexible system. However, this relies on an electricity supply, although it can be used in conjunction with a landline telephone system. This was first done with the Minehead-Blue Anchor section, with

An atmospheric shot as a double-headed train climbs out of Watchet. (Steve Edge)

Visiting 4-6-0 Ex-L.M.S. 6100 Royal Scot *leaves Blue Anchor for Minehead with a service train.* 29 March 2009. (Steve Edge)

the staff and ticket system remaining for the rest of the line. The system is known as electric key token (EKT), although the G.W.R. called it the electric train token (ETT). A number of aluminium key tokens, again shaped and coloured in a different way for each section, so that they only fit the instruments at each end of the section, are kept in special instruments and since there are a number of these in each instrument, trains can be sent up and down at will. The instruments are operated by means of special bell codes.

Meanwhile, miracles of engineering are performed in Minehead loco shed, where one locomotive has been completely rebuilt. Ex-G.W.R. 2-6-2 tank No. 5391 was converted into a 2-6-0 tender engine, similar, though not identical, to those which ran on the line for many years in former days. It has proved an ideal addition to the railway's motive power. Most people are unaware that a locomotive's boiler is only certificated for ten years; after that it has to come out of service for a complete overhaul. For this reason, some are disappointed that a locomotive they particularly wanted to see is not available. However, the railway does not want its passengers moved upwards, rather than forwards! An enormous amount of work goes on behind the scenes to enable the railway to run. The permanent way gangs are constantly about on the line doing such unglamorous work as replacing worn-out sleepers (on which the rails rest), repairing fencing, relaying lengths of rail and similar tasks, often in very inclement weather. There is also the cutting back gang, who devote a large part of their lives keeping the lineside jungle in check, so that passengers may enjoy the unrivalled views from their seats. These, too, are out in all weathers and the two gangs occasionally join up for an especially heavy task.

The West Somerset Railway, now one of the United Kingdom's pre-eminent heritage railways, is probably looking its best since it was built. Negotiations are ongoing with a view to establishing a link with Taunton, probably from Bishops Lydeard. W.S.R. trains are unable to run through owing to them not being maintained to main-line standards and they would have to run on the main West of England line. However, outside operators can, and do, run on to the W.S.R. and such a link would at last fulfil the dreams of those early pioneers who struggled so hard to reopen the line all those years ago.

GWR 2-6-2 No. 5542 with an auto-train at Muddymoor. (Steve Edge)

Taunton to Bishops Lydeard shuttle at Longlands Bridge. 9 October 2016. (Steve Edge)

Bampton Station in 1962, with loco 1462 and auto-train waiting to leave for Exeter. (M.J. Fox)

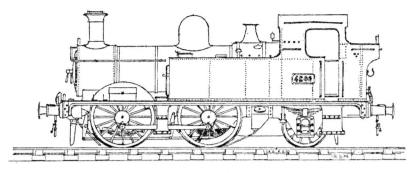

4800. GWR 0–4-2T for 'auto-coach' working.

Exe Valley

This line, one of three operated by the G.W.R. and included in this book, was perhaps the sleepiest and most picturesque of all, as it ran for much of its 24 miles beside the River Exe. As so often happened, the history of the line was complicated, since it started as two separate ventures and these in turn linked with a third, with Tiverton as the focal town.

History

Chronologically, the first railway to reach Tiverton was the branch from Tiverton Junction (or Tiverton Road as it was first called), constructed by the Bristol and Exeter and opened on 12 June 1848. This was laid as a broad gauge line but converted to standard on 29 June 1884, in anticipation of the opening of the Exe Valley line, standard from the start. Just under 5 miles long, the branch had no crossing loops and only one intermediate station at Halberton, where it passed beneath the Great Western Canal, built in the early 1800s to link the River Exe at Tiverton with the River Tone in the vicinity of Greenham, about 6 miles west of Wellington. Two separate arches under the canal indicated the intention to double-track. The train was operated as a shuttle service and known familiarly as the 'Tivvy Bumper'.

The Exe Valley Railway, so-called, was authorised in 1874 to connect Tiverton with the West of England main line at Stoke Canon, 3½ miles north of Exeter, and opened on 1 May 1885. The B. & E.R. was to be the operating company but as the latter was leased to the G.W.R. in 1876, the new line followed suit at once. As to the extension north of Tiverton, this section, following the Exe

Thorverton Station.

at the beginning and end of its route with a 'leg' through Bampton, was built by a different concern, the Exe Valley North Railway. It reached Dulverton via a junction with the Taunton-Barnstaple line at Morebath and such was the expedition of the Liverpool contractor, Nathaniel B. Fogg, that it was opened on 1 August 1884, some nine months before the completion of the southern section. When the line was open for its whole length, the old B. & E.R. terminal station at Tiverton was relegated to the status of a goods shed and a new station was put up. Although worked as a single unit all through by the G.W.R., the northern section retained its nominal independence for twenty years under the name of the Tiverton and North Devon Railway.

Route – southern section

At Exeter St David's, finding the Exe Valley train was quite a feat; but once aboard and provided you were in no hurry, you could look forward to a delightful and leisurely run. The first stop, Stoke Canon (rebuilt twice in 1894 and 1932), consisted of two platforms serving the relief lines where slower trains could be held to allow fast traffic to pass. The up platform had an outside face for the branch line trains, which, to reach Exeter, had to cross over on to the main line and were often delayed as a result. From Stoke Canon, the branch line curved away northwards to Bramford Speke Halt, about a mile on, and soon after crossed the River Exe before reaching

Thorverton, with its passing loop and goods shed on a further loop behind the down platform. Incidentally, there was a loading gauge at either end of this siding and another siding to a mill, which once provided grain traffic for the branch. The generous layout and equipment were all evidence of a thriving past. Further on, the level crossings on either side of the Up Exe Halt were protected by distant signals in both directions. The signal levers were interlocked with the gate locking levers in the adjoining ground frames and so it was not uncommon for these signals to show a clear indication in either direction, even though the line was single track at this point.

Between Up Exe and Burn Halt, the valley is still wide, with the river meandering through the meadows and offering some excellent fishing. James Connell, a keen angler, recalled:

0.4.2T. No.1451 with the Exe Valley line train arriving at Tiverton Station. (R.E. Toop)

Morebath Halt.

The Amory Hounds being unboxed at Dulverton Station, c. 1910.
(Dulverton Heritage Centre)

'By kind permission of Sir John Amory I have fished many times below Burn Halt, where there are some fine salmon pools and good trout runs. The river is deep down there, and one way of crossing from bank to bank is by a little suspension bridge which swings perilously as you walk over it. About twenty feet below, I have often looked into a deep pool full of gigantic trout but like all trout under a bridge, how difficult they are to tempt to the fly!'

Soon the valley closes in, with the railway, river and adjoining road converging to a point where they all crossed each other at Bickleigh, a pretty little hamlet of thatched cottages and an inn, and an awkward sixteenth-century stone bridge to complete the picture. To avoid confusion with the Bickleigh, near Plymouth, the station was called Cadeleigh; but this village was some 3 miles away, so one confusion replaced another. The station was well provided with a passing loop and a goods yard and, as at Thorverton, the signal box was sited on the platform itself. Running north again, through beautiful wooded country, road and rail kept close together: the proximity proving so tempting that, since the line closed, the highway authority has used part of the track foundation for road improvement. Tiverton West Exe was once a busy halt for passenger traffic; thereafter the line ran across the southern part of the town to the main station, crossing the Exe yet again *en route*. Tiverton Station had two platforms connected by a footbridge and a separate bay on the down platform for the branch trains to the junction. An extensive goods yard was laid out on the up side, together with sidings for the gasworks, petroleum tanks and several coal depots.

Route – northern section

First stop after Tiverton was Bolham Halt, actually at Bolham, a charming village with wisteria clinging to the walls of the houses and close to Knightshayes, famous for its gardens, the property of the Heathcoat Amory family, long connected with industry and public life in Tiverton. Half a mile on, the line re-joined the river by a series of weirs; thereafter road and rail hugged the east side of the narrowing valley, between thickly wooded slopes with brief glimpses of lonely cottages and farmhouses perched high among the trees. Cove looked busier than it really was, by reason of the dust and clatter from the quarry hard by. The halt was simply a single platform, meagrely equipped, and the mechanism controlling the level crossing was not even a separate 'block post', the signal having to rely on the bell codes passing between Bampton and Tiverton to give warning when trains were due. The siding had

Exe Valley auto-train at Dulverton. First coach is 'Thrush' No. 221. (M.J. Fox)

a total capacity of three trucks! But the acoustics were good, for Bampton people used to say that if you could hear the train leaving Cove Halt, then rain was on the way; and very often they were right. The pagoda shelter formerly at Cove now does duty at Doniford Halt on the West Somerset Railway.

Hard by the Exeter Inn, the railway exchanged the River Exe for the Batherm and followed the latter into Bampton; a quiet country town, a centre for stone quarrying but best known, perhaps, for its pony fair held on the last Thursday in October. On that day, the streets are lined with stalls, traffic can hardly move and, before the days of road transport, the railway did a roaring trade in pony haulage. But the station, with its two platforms, modest buildings and goods yard, is dead now; and so is the final stretch of track past the level crossing at Lower Lodfin, so often shut when nothing more dangerous than the trolley was expected in ten minutes' time, before the junction at Morebath. Thence it was a few minutes run into the terminus at Dulverton, after finding and crossing the Exe once again close by Blackpool, the famous fishing spot formed by the confluence of the Exe and the Barle.

Engines and rolling stock

The maximum speed permitted on the branch was 35 miles per hour and the entire journey of some 24 miles took about eighty minutes; not so much a journey as a rest cure. The line was worked for the most part by that typical

G.W.R. institution, the 'auto-train', the engine normally heading the train to Dulverton and pushing it back to Exeter. At the end of the leading coach was a special compartment for the driver, his mate occupying the engine, the train being operated by controls between the forward cabin and the engine cab. A huge gong controlled by a foot pedal gave warning of the train's approach. Some of this stock had been converted from steam rail-motor coaches. These had a small, vertical boiler and two diminutive cylinders, operated by Walschaert's valve-gear carried on one bogie and taking up a large part of one end of the coach, along with the driving compartment. A second driving compartment was at the other end. A simple conversion entailed replacing the 'power' bogie with a standard coach bogie, the resulting space being turned into a luggage compartment. These 'auto-coaches' were so popular that some were even built under B.R. ownership and in an effort to increase their popularity, a few were given birds' names. One of them, 'Thrush', worked the line in its last months.

The engines of push-pull trains were of the 14XX 0-4-2T class, diminutive, yet handsome. Fortunately, No. 1442 has been preserved by the generosity of Lord Amory and stands in the Tiverton museum, resplendent in G.W.R. livery. Working examples of this class still do yeoman service on the South Devon Railway and delight thousands of holidaymakers with the opportunity of riding behind a steam engine. Occasionally, some of the 64XX 0-6-0 pannier tanks, also fitted for auto-working, were used on the line. The 45XX 2-6-2Ts also appeared with G.W.R. suburban non-corridor stock and towards the end, some of the 57ft. bow-ended main line coaches ended their lives here.

Until the very end of the line, there was an adequate passenger service of some nine trains each way on weekdays and a reduced service between Exeter and Tiverton only on summer Sundays. Goods traffic had been light for many years, about a single journey a day in each direction. When closure came, it came piecemeal: first the section Morebath-Thorverton on 7 October 1963, except for Tiverton-West Exe and Tiverton-Tiverton junction. For a time, the Tiverton-West Exe section was used as a storage siding for surplus goods wagons until the scrap yards could take them. The remainder of the route, Thorverton-Stoke Canon, was closed on 30 November 1966. Finally, the Tiverton-Tiverton junction section came to an end of 7 July 1967. As this had been the first part of the line to be opened, closing it last was historical justice.

On the tough 1 in 36 out of Ilfracombe, a train for Exeter climbs to Mortehoe, headed by Battle of Britain Class 4-6-2 locomotives 34058 Sir Frederick Pile (pilot) and 34052 Lord Dowding.
(S. Creer)

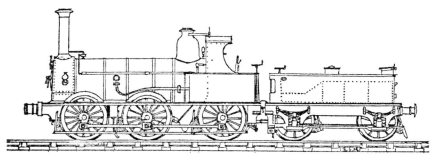

B. & I. 0-6-0 'Ilfracombe' goods.

Barnstaple – Ilfracombe

For many people, not only railway enthusiasts, the West Country is synonymous with the G.W.R., so it comes as a shock to find that the lines serving the North Devon coast and most of the North Cornish coast, too, were exclusively S.R.; the latter having inherited them from one of its constituent companies: the L. & S.W.R. The Barnstaple-Ilfracombe branch, at the north-west corner of the S.R. system belonged, geographically, to the 'railways round Exmoor'.

History

Chronologically, we must begin at Exeter St David's, reached in 1844 by the Bristol and Exeter Railway, a broad gauge line (later G.W.R.), some sixteen years ahead of the L & S.W.R., which only struggled through to Exeter Queen Street (now Central) after piecemeal acquisition of lines south and west of Basingstoke. West of Exeter, the story of railway development is so confusing as almost to defy description, a miserable episode in the war of the gauges. Suffice it to say that, after much delay and doubtful dealing, a broad gauge line was opened from Exeter (*via* Cowley Bridge junction) to Crediton in 1847, then narrowed to standard, then left unused. Next, the broad was re-laid alongside the standard and the route to Crediton opened in 1851, but with trains running single line on the broad gauge only. Three years later, the Crediton-Barnstaple section was ready and the through route from Exeter operated on a mixed gauge as from 1 August 1854. Finally, in 1862-3 the L. & S.W.R. took steps to acquire the whole concern, although the G.W.R.

retained running rights for a number of years to come. Broad gauge did not disappear until the general gauge conversion in 1892.

Although in this instance the L. & S.W.R. came out on top and at the same time strengthened its hold on the south-west by extensions to Bideford and Torrington, and by pushing other lines through to the Atlantic coast further south, all the delays and complications involved had done serious damage to the potential of trade and tourism in North Devon. Besides this, the line to Barnstaple was limited in capacity. Much of it was single track, with inadequate signalling and passing places, while the train service was infrequent. Most of these disadvantages applied to the Ilfracombe branch, which suffered many setbacks both before and during construction. As Jim Lock relates in his account, written for the centenary of the line, 1874-1974 (North Devon Railway Preservation Society), active steps to extend the railway from Barnstaple to Ilfracombe were taken by an Exeter solicitor, Robert Wreford, soon after 1854. Then,

'In 1860 a local committee was formed to try to find the best route … Two routes were suggested. The eastern or Bittadon route which from Barnstaple went almost due north through Bittadon to cross a range of hills at 800 ft., entering Ilfracombe from the east to terminate above the harbour. The western or Braunton route left Barnstaple in a westerly direction to follow the north bank of the Taw, then turning inland to Braunton, crossing the hills at a lower level than the Bittadon route before terminating above the town of Ilfracombe.

'The latter route was finally selected, the eastern route being rejected as too expensive. Great opposition to the western route was put forward by the Lord of the Manor, Sir William Williams, who owned Heanton Court, as the line would run between his property and the river. Another problem at this time was the apparent apathy of the residents of Ilfracombe'.

Successive attempts to promote the scheme all failed during the 1860s. The Devon and Somerset Railway Company agreed to extend its Taunton-Barnstaple track but failed to find the money; while a proposal by L. & S.W.R. for a light railway and a bridge over the Taw downstream of Heanton Court also came to nothing. Ultimately, Sir William Williams withdrew his opposition to the Braunton route and in March 1870, the Barnstaple and Ilfracombe Railway Company (a L. & S.W.R. subsidiary) received powers to build the line.

Southern Class N2-6-0 No. 31841 with an up freight train crossing the River Taw at Barnstaple. The bridge is now demolished. (R.E.Toop)

'When gentlemen of Ilfracombe, the Rev. W.C. Moore and the Rev. B. Price, together with Messrs. W.R. Gould and P. Stoneman arrived home after attending Parliament, the omnibus which had collected them from Barnstaple was met outside Ilfracombe, the horses unhitched and the vehicle drawn by men through the streets amidst tremendous cheering. On March 24th, the death of Sir William Williams occurred at Tregulla in Cornwall, only one week after he had conceded victory'.

Four more years were to elapse before the line was completed. Construction encountered all kinds of difficulties, mainly a lack of labour and some formidable engineering problems, including heavy gradients, sharp curves and a number of bridges, embankments and cuttings for most of the way along the 15-mile route. The track was doubled between 1889 and 1891.

Route
From Barnstaple Junction to the town station the single track line took the shape of an inverted S and crossed the River Taw by a girder bridge remark-

Ex-SEC class N 2-6-0 No31837 entering Wrafton with the 17.15 train from Barnstaple on 21 July 1964. At this time most, if not all, engines in this area were filthy dirty. (Roger Palmer)

On Mortehoe Bank. (P. Waylett)

Engine No. 31837 at Mortehoe & Woolacombe Station with 17.15 Barnstaple to Ilfracombe. Photographed on 21 July 1964. (Roger Palmer)

able for its sharp curvature at the northern end. Thereafter it ran double track (latterly singled) beside the estuary as far as the approaches to Chivenor, with delightful views over the sand and water flats towards the south shore at Penhill Point. The next section inland must have been no less attractive before the construction of Chivenor as an R.A.F. station and the spread of suburban housing at Wrafton and Braunton, now appendages of Barnstaple. North of Braunton, however, the crowding declines and the line passed along the delightfully wooded valley of the River Caen, peppered with farms and cottages and interrupted by frequent level crossings. At the end of the valley, the serious work began, and for 3 miles the line struggled up a heavy gradient of 1 in 40, swinging sharply north-west through several embankments and cuttings to reach Mortehoe and Woolacombe Station at 600 feet above sea level. It then continued its tortuous route, descending 2 miles at 1 in 36, heavily engineered, to reach Ilfracombe on a magnificent artificial plateau above the town.

Service

Although the SR route to Exeter was shorter than the G.W.R., the latter was faster by nearly half-an-hour. However, the S.R. made much of its main train of the day to the south-west: the 'Atlantic Coast Express' (ACE), which left Waterloo at 11.0 a.m. and comprised no fewer than nine sections, each of one coach, a composite brake, except for the Ilfracombe portion, which had two third-class brakes and a first-third composite between them. The formation was three coaches for Ilfracombe, then one each for Bideford, Torrington, Plymouth, Padstow, Bude, two restaurant cars and a coach for Exeter, and coaches for Sidmouth and Exmouth detached at Sidmouth Junction. Thus, this train had more sections than any other named train in the country. Incidentally, the G.W.R. also provided a through service to Ilfracombe, by means of a slip-coach detached from the 'Cornish Riviera Express' at Taunton. In 1947, the S.R. and the Pullman Car Company introduced the 'Devon Belle', a luxury train complete with observation car. The venture did not prove a success, however, and was abandoned after the 1954 season.

Engines

The gradients of the line west of Exeter and the weight restrictions of the permanent way have always been conflicting factors difficult to resolve in terms of engine power. Successive engineers of the L.S.W.R. and S.R wrestled with the problem and some very handsome, though moderately–sized engines resulted. With the railway grouping of 1923, R.E.L. Maunsell of the old South Eastern and Chatham Railway took charge and, so far as the lines in North Devon were concerned, his N class 2-6-0 locomotives were in general use. When O.V.S. Bulleid succeeded Maunsell in 1937, the engine state of the S.R. was becoming critical. The heavy loading of the Waterloo-Exeter expresses was almost beyond the capabilities of the 'King Arthurs' and the few 'Lord Nelsons' then available, while further west a multiplicity of designs left over from before 1923 posed problems of maintenance and spares. Accordingly, Bulleid produced a revolutionary 4-6-2 main line locomotive with streamline casing, the first Pacific design ever on the S.R. These engines did not start work until 1941 and S.R. loco men dubbed them 'Spam cans'. Officially known as the 'Merchant Navy' class, they were followed by the 'West Country' class, similar in externals and all bearing west country place names. The advantage of the latter class was that it combined express capability with such a light axle-loading that the engines soon found their way on to the Ilfracombe branch and handled nearly all the principal passenger trains. Later, under B.R., both engine classes were rebuilt with improved valve gear and without the streamline casing.

Mention should also be made of an early design, in 1873, by Beyer, Peacock, for an 0-6-0 tender engine which came to be known as the 'Ilfracombe Goods'. It was so successful that the makers furnished several other railways with the same design, so that examples (new or second hand) could be seen as far away as on the Shropshire & Montgomeryshire Railway and the Kent & East Sussex Railway, also overseas in Sweden.

Once steam traction had been withdrawn, the regular services were run with diesel 2- or 3-car units operating locally from Barnstaple but the daily London trains were hauled by 'Warship' class locomotives. Goods were mostly handled by 63XX diesel-hydraulics of the Western Region, to which the branch was transferred before final closure on 5 October 1970.

Revival?

As in the case of the West Somerset Railway, no sooner had the line been closed than proposals were advanced for reopening under private management. By 1974, the North Devon Railway Co. Ltd. had been formed and about £20,000 raised for the project. However, in 1975 British Railways lifted all the rails and gave orders for the removal of the curved girder bridge across the River Taw. This was accomplished by 1977 and meant that any attempt to revive the line would result in its having no physical connection with the B.R. town station, whilst development put paid to any possibility of reopening the line to Ilfracombe. In any event, maintenance of the girder bridge would have proved a considerable drain on the company's resources in the course of time.

Most of the supporters of the project transferred their allegiance to other heritage projects in the area, such as the West Somerset Railway and the very attractive restored signal box and its environs at Instow on the former line to Torrington. The possibility of restoration of the line from Barnstaple to Bideford and even Torrington is still regularly aired.

Lyd, autumn 2015. (Tony Nicholson)

The Lyd is a "Lynton & Barnstaple Railway Class" locomotive, owned and operated by the Ffestiniog and Welsh Highland Railway, but a frequent visitor to the line.

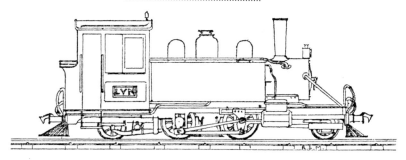

L. & B. 2-4-2T 'Lyn', "The Yankee".

Lynton – Barnstaple

The story of the Lynton and Barnstaple Railway is one of tragedy to triumph. Closed on 30 September 1935, one of the earlier closures of the country's narrow gauge railways, it appears to have been held in genuine affection by those who used it and lived close by. There was much opposition to its closure but to the Southern Railway, which inherited it on the grouping in 1923, it was an anachronism. Like many other lines, creative accounting and inconvenient timetabling gave the S.R. the excuse it needed to close the line. The day after the last train ran, Barnstaple Town Stationmaster Harold Ford and Porter Guard George Walkey laid a wreath of bronze chrysanthemums on the Barnstaple Station stop block. Sent by Paymaster Captain Thomas Alfred Woolf, R.N. (Retired.) of the White House Woody Bay, written on a black-edged postcard attached to the wreath were these words "Perchance it is not dead but sleepeth". The Captain could not possibly have known how prescient these words were.

History

Exmoor's wild countryside was untouched by the tourist until the early nineteenth century, when the impossibility of travelling on the continent, owing to the Napoleonic wars and the growth of romantic interest in grand scenery, induced a few visitors to make hazardous journeys along the coast and rent rooms for holidays in fishing villages such as Porlock and Lynmouth. Others came by sea, as indeed did most trade, but the real development of trade and tourism sprang out of the southward extension of the railway from Bristol in the 1840s and the opening of the North Devon Railway from Exeter to Barnsta-

Budds Wood. (D.E.H. Box)

Last train at Rowley Bank. (R.L. Knight)

ple in 1854, followed by connecting coach services, Bridgwater-Minehead-Lynton and Barnstaple-Ilfracombe-Combe Martin-Lynton.

The railway network continued to spread *round* Exmoor, with the opening of the Taunton-Barnstaple and Taunton-Minehead lines in 1873 and 1874 and of the Barnstaple-Ilfracombe line in 1874. Coaches collected passengers either from the termini or from intermediate stations, so that well before the railway reached Lynton, this part of the coast had become comparatively accessible and popular, with much renown attaching to some of the coach teams. Even so, travel was slow; most of the coach runs to Lynton taking up to three hours.

For this reason pressure for a railway never relaxed. The two nearest main line companies, the G.W.R and the L.S.W.R., examined various proposals but in the end they refused to take action on the grounds that the district was too sparsely populated to produce sufficient revenue. Other local undertakings, usually favouring a coastal route *via* Ilfracombe and Combe Martin, also came to nothing. In 1882, sanction was sought for a tramway from Lynton *via* Blackmoor Gate to Braunton and thence over L.S.W.R. metals to Barnstaple, the line to be called the Barnstaple and Lynton Electric Tramroad Company. This scheme, too, was abandoned.

Hitherto, planning had generally been in terms of standard gauge but now a group of local gentry, led by Sir George Newnes (the publisher), who had settled at Lynton, began to canvass the advantages of narrow gauge. Their arguments were reinforced by the obvious success of similar lines in Wales: the Festiniog, the Corris Railway and the North Wales Narrow Gauge Railway (later to become the Welsh Highland Railway). It was claimed that the narrow gauge (1ft. 11½ins.) would cost less to construct in hilly country; you could take liberties with curves and contours and economise with cuttings and embankments and that this offset any inconvenience caused by a break of gauge, where the line met the standard gauge. At the same time, a rival syndicate, headed by Lord Fortescue, revived interest in a variation of an earlier scheme for a standard gauge branch from Filleigh, to which the G.W.R. now lent its support. However, the influence of Sir George Newnes eventually told in favour of the narrow gauge plan, with the result that the Royal Assent was given to the Lynton and Barnstaple Railway Bill on 27 June 1895.

Construction began with high hopes. Sir James Szlumper was appointed consultant engineer and a group of local residents took up leading positions as directors or executives, notably F.W. Chanter, whose job it was to survey the route and who was later appointed engineer and general manager. As usual, actual outlay far exceeded initial estimates and there were any number of unexpected difficulties. Some of the landowners stood out for higher prices than anticipated. At Barnstaple there were complaints about the proposed level crossings, while for a long time the L.S.W.R. objected to the L. & B.R. using Barnstaple Town Station as its terminus. At Lynton, the fact that the station involved a climb of 250 feet up from the town proved a lasting and damaging drawback. But the main trouble was due to the optimism of the surveyors in assuming that construction would entail no more than the removal of a surface layer of soil, though to anyone examining the outcrops of stone along the route, this would have patently seemed a pious hope. Eventually, construction worked out at £5000 per mile, double the original estimate; the contractor, James Nuttall of Manchester, suffered severe financial difficulties; there was an expensive lawsuit and the company never raised sufficient money to give itself a chance.

However, in spite of everything, the line was eventually ready by May 1898. The Board of Trade inspection went well and the formal opening on 11 May

Entering Woody Bay. (R.L. Knight)

Chelfham Viaduct. (Major Darker and Loraine)

Yeo at Barnstaple Town Station. (R.L. Knight)

was an undoubted triumph with two trains packed with VIPs, speeches, a triumphal arch at Bratton and red, white and blue ribbons cut by Lady Newnes at Lynton, where the lifeboat crew turned out to do honour.

Route

At Barnstaple Town, the L. & B.R. had a bay to itself, the first train on the summer timetable leaving about 6.20 a.m., to be followed by half-a-dozen more before the end of the day. The line curved away almost at once, following North Walk, crossed Braunton Road and Pilton Road, both on the level, and then passed Pilton yard, the depot of the company, which was furnished with engine and carriage sheds, offices and a goods yard. After Barnstaple, it was all country, at first along the valley of the River Yeo, which the line crossed four times in all. Snapper Halt, at Yeotown, west of Goodleigh, came after 2½ miles, consisting of a shed and a single platform adjacent to the main road. Soon afterwards, the line began to climb in earnest and for the next 8 miles or so, the gradient ranged around 1 in 50, with frequent changes of direction as the route wound along the narrow and pleas- antly wooded valley. In due course, a prolonged curve brought Chelfham Viaduct into view, the biggest engineering feature of the line, built to span the Stoke Rivers valley where it joined the Yeo from the east.

Chelfham Station (pronounced Chilham locally) lay immediately beyond the viaduct, partly concealed by trees planted by the builders and facing Youlston wood over the river, a favourite haunt of wild red deer. The station had a passing loop with two platforms, a stone-built waiting room and a water tank for topping up the locomotives. It was here that a typical branch incident took place many years ago. The engine of an up train for Barnstaple had to be detached for shunting. The job done, it continued on its way, to arrive at its destination only to find that it had left the passenger coaches behind at Chelfham. What the passengers, if any, and the guard said, while they awaited the engine's return is not recorded!

Soon after leaving Chelfham, the line abandoned the Yeo valley and turned north-east into the more rugged terrain leading to Bratton Fleming. This was a very tortuous section with rock cuttings and embankments, several culverts, another smaller viaduct over Lancey Brook and, shortly before Bratton, a small quarry used to supply ballast for the track. The station, a steep walk from Bratton Fleming village, originally had a passing loop but this was

Lyn *at Quarry Bridge.* (D.E.H. Box)

Down train near Narracott. (F.E. Box)

removed in 1912 leaving one long siding half way along the platform length. It was a pretty place, with shrubs and flowers and quite an important stop. For a while, the gradient eased but the hard going soon returned, while the train snorted past hidden farms with the lovely Devon names of Knightacott, Narracott, Sprecott and Hunnacott. This section, with its succession of high cuttings and embankments, gave the engines more trouble, perhaps, than any other portion of the track and it is just north of here that a short section of the line has now been drowned by the construction of Wistlandpound Reservoir. At the top end the route can be picked up again as it curved round the high bluff of Wistlandpound Farm and so into Blackmoor Station on the Barnstaple side of the cross-roads and a little over half-way towards Lynton. Since it was intended as the main intermediate station on the line, connecting with coaches from Ilfracombe, the building and lay-out were quite elaborate, with refreshment rooms (the main building still serves as a restaurant), stables and a goods yard.

The gradient fell away beyond Blackmoor, the line skirting Parracombe by a generous curve before climbing again at 1 in 50 to reach the halt close to the

Blackmoor Station from the south, 1935. (G.N. Southerden)

Lynton Station, 1924. (H.R. Norman)

old church of St Petrock, remarkable for its Georgian furnishings. The Rev. J.F. Chanter, a former rector, amateur antiquary and something of a Devon character, used to scatter flower seeds from the carriage window for bright blooms in summer. Engines watered here before attacking the final 1½ miles up to the summit of the railway at Woody Bay, 980 feet above sea level. The station was close to Martinhoe Cross, some two miles from the sea and the site of an abortive attempt to develop a resort.

There was not now far to go. The line emerged from a steep cutting on to the hillside with a wonderful view south-eastwards over West Ilkerton Common towards the Exmoor hills. It then brushed past Caffyns Halt, turned right-handed down Dean Steep to Barbrook, whence it dropped down through the woods into Lynton Station, at 700 feet. The 19½ mile journey had taken about an hour and a half. It rarely took less.

Engines and rolling stock

Owing to lack of funds, the L. & B.R. never had more than a minimum of equipment and even after its absorption by the Southern Railway in 1923, it was not rich in this respect. At the outset, the company bought three

Early view of Yeo *in Pilton Yard.* (Major Darker and Loraine)

Lew *ready for last train, 29 September 1935.* (D.E.H. Box)

Manning Wardle 2-6-2Ts named *Yeo*, *Exe* and *Taw*, and soon after a Baldwin locomotive of similar type, only of 2-4-2T wheel arrangement, from America named *Lyn*. All were well maintained and sported a sombre livery of holly green, edged with black and orange, against which the brass dome and other fittings showed up splendidly. In 1925, the S.R. purchased another Manning, Wardle, *Lew*, and altered the colour scheme. The majority of the passenger coaches were built at Bristol, strong, rather primitive-looking vehicles with wooden bodies on composite frames, lit first by oil and then by acetylene. Unfortunately, the roller bearings initially fitted, suffered uneven wear and although the coaches were turned round periodically, the trouble continued so that in the end plain bearings had to be substituted. Although passenger traffic did well in the summer and on market days, it never was sufficient to carry the line throughout the year. Goods were an important part of the business of the line, at least until the development of motor lorries between the wars, with coal as the chief item. After the line closed, the price of coal delivered to Lynton and intermediate stations rose noticeably in price. But there was quite a brisk trade outwards in household and farm supplies and ordinary parcels, although the return loading never amounted to very much.

The last years

The L. & B.R. made most profit in 1913 and 1919, when it paid a dividend of ½%. In 1922, it barely broke even and sold out to the L.S.W.R. which, in the following year, became part of the S.R. Thanks to a series of improvements, the line underwent a marked rejuvenation. Maintenance was made up in various ways, the track renovated, new signalling installed here and there, engines and rolling stock overhauled, some new units purchased and the buildings at Lynton enlarged. But by the late 1920s, competition from motor traffic was beginning to tell and thereafter the line ran regularly at a loss. Economies followed until, with fewer and fewer people using the line, final closure was announced for the end of the summer season of 1935. At the decisive conference, held on 11 April in Barnstaple, it was revealed that the great majority of objectors had come by car as there was no late train!

Phoenix

The Lynton and Barnstaple has always been a kind of Cinderella among narrow gauge railways, particularly since its original closure in 1935. It was by far the longest public narrow gauge railway in mainland Britain and it

Isaac near Woody Bay. (Andrew Curry)

was unusual in that, from its conception, it was designed principally as a passenger-carrying line, unlike most of the others, the origins of which stemmed from industry of one sort or another. Ever since its closure, people have nurtured an idea that it might somehow be possible to resurrect it, or part of it. After closure, the track was swiftly lifted and it, the locomotives and rolling stock and the majority of the infrastructure had been sold off within three years.

Probably inspired by the success of the revived Welsh narrow gauge lines, a Lynton and Barnstaple Railway Society was formed in 1962 but when the cost of restoring just a small section of it became apparent, the Society decided it was unaffordable with the resources then at their disposal and the Society was disbanded two years later. A major difficulty which faced the Society was that, unlike some other similar projects, the track bed had been sold to a multitude of different landowners and acquiring it would prove to be a costly and probably long drawn out business.

In 1979, it was decided to have another try and the Lynton and Barnstaple Railway Association (replaced by a charitable trust in 2000) was founded.

Lyd *2014 Autumn Gala.* (Pete Snashall)

Their aim was to attempt to reopen as much of the old line as possible and to this end, as soon as sufficient funds had been accumulated, the Association purchased Woody Bay Station in 1995. In the meantime, they had been operating a narrow gauge line, called the Lynbarn Railway, at the Milky Way Adventure Park near Clovelly in order to raise funds and obtain practical operating experience in working a real railway, ready for the day, it was hoped, that they would be able to run trains from Woody Bay Station. The Lynbarn Railway was sold to the Milky Way Adventure Park in 2005, as it had fulfilled its purpose.

Members and supporters have always kept a keen eye on the local land and property sales scene and have been swift to snap up the different parts of the track bed as it has become available over the years. The result has been that a good deal of the track bed is now in the hands of either the trust, associated organisations or supportive individuals, though the sections are usually widely spaced out. One such acquisition has been Chelfham Station and the Station Master's house, Distant Point; the former serendipitously left standing upon the abandonment of the line. Chelfham Viaduct, now owned by the Highways

Lyd entering Woody Bay 2016. (Keith Vingoe)

Agency, was fully restored to train-carrying standard by the British Railways Board (Residuary) Ltd in 2000. 2002 saw the first track laid at Woody Bay, with the station being opened as a visitor centre the following year and on 17 July 2004, the first passenger train for over seventy years left Woody Bay Station. On 27 May 2006 the line was extended to Killington Lane, about a mile away. In 2016, planning applications were submitted to extend the line from Killington Lane to Blackmoor (formerly Blackmoor Gate) and Wistland-pound. This would add about 4 miles to the existing line and it is intended that the main depot of the line will move from Woody Bay to Blackmoor in due course.

Wistlandpound, where a reservoir was constructed after closure, flooding a small section of the track bed, will pose a slight but not insurmountable challenge. After all, the Ffestiniog faced a similar challenge and managed to surmount it magnificently. The Lynton & Barnstaple Trust's current aim is to restore the whole line from Lynton to Barnstaple. Almost all of the original buildings survive, although they have now been converted to other uses. Probably the most notable are Lynton Station House (now a private residence), Woody Bay Station and Blackmoor Station (currently an inn). Restoration of the whole route would undoubtedly contribute enormously to tourism in North Devon and the western fringes of Exmoor, through which the line runs from Blackmoor to Lynton, about half the total length of the line. 51,000 passengers travelled on the line in 2016.

Locomotives and rolling stock

All the locomotives were sold at auction in November 1935. All, save *Lew*, were scrapped. *Lew* was reputedly sold to a plantation in Brazil and subsequently lost to view. Two carriages were sold at the auction and the remainder were later either smashed and burned or sectioned and sold off as garden sheds. The Trust has, perforce, had to rely on hiring or borrowing outside motive power as well as passenger carriages. Currently on the line are three locomotives: 0-6-0T *Axe*, a Kerr, Stuart locomotive built in 1915 but totally rebuilt at the Gartell Light Railway (at Templecombe) in 2009. The two others, both owned by members, are *Isaac*, a Bagnall 0-4-2T of 1953 and *Charles Wytock* a Bagnall 4-4-0T built in 1946. It is the intention that the line should eventually have five replica locomotives of those originally used on the line and to that end, the 762 club was formed in 2009 to fund the construction of a replica 2-4-2T similar to No. 762, the Baldwin engine which ran on the line. It is hoped this will enter service in the spring of 2017. Meanwhile, *Lyd*, a loco built by the Ffestiniog Railway to the design of "Lynton & Barnstaple Railway Class" locomotives, constructed by Manning Wardle, has been a frequent visitor to the line. It is owned and operated by the Ffestiniog and Welsh Highland Railway.

Of the two original passenger carriages that survived, carriage No.15 (S.R 6993) was rescued from Snapper Halt, where it had lain since closure, by the Ffestiniog Railway in 1959. It was converted into a Buffet Car and has run there ever since as their No.14. In 1982, coach no. 2 (S.R 6992) was moved from Clannaborough Rectory, where it had been since closure, to the National Railway Museum at York, where it has been exhibited in 'as found' condition ever since and a wonderful exhibit it is.

Eight carriages were acquired in the early 1990s from the Thorpe Park Theme Park in Surrey. Three of these vehicles entered service on the Lynbarn Railway at the Milky Way in 1994/95. The others were put in store until such time as they were required at Woody Bay. Four of these were eventually rebuilt and served well. However, the intention was always to operate with L&B style carriages.

Isaac and Lyd on an up train at bridge 67. (Will Curry)

Carriage starts its downward journey. (Rev. W.A. Bevis)

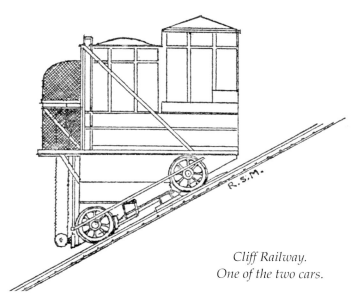

Cliff Railway.
One of the two cars.

Lynton – Lynmouth

Lynton and Lynmouth are separated and distinguished by a simple but fearsome feature of geography; a cliff, 500 feet high, rising sheer out of the sea, with Lynton at the top and Lynmouth at the bottom. The shortest road between the two has gradients steeper than 1 in 4, a formidable barrier today but an even more effective deterrent to the carriage of persons and goods before the days of cars, when the only alternative was the valley road round, about 5 miles long.

History

It is not known who first suggested the idea of a funicular railway linking Lynton and Lynmouth. It was part of a scheme to build an esplanade at Lynmouth, together with a pier to encourage ships plying the Bristol Channel to call at the port bringing boatloads of tourists to boost the local economy. Bob Jones, a local builder, recommended his sister's son, George Marks, as an engineer with the necessary skills needed to advise on the project.

Marks realised that with the line rising over 500 ft. vertically at an incline of 1:1.75, safety was of paramount importance. Accordingly, he adopted four

The lines diverge halfway to allow the carriages to pass. (Robin Madge)

separate braking systems. Two were friction brakes, in which sets of steel blocks are pressed down on to the crown of the rails by hydraulic pressure. The main system was hydraulic callipers which clamped across the crown of the rails. This hydraulic system was filled with water and not the more customary oil.

A major drawback faced by the promoters of the cliff railway scheme was the amount of capital required to build it. Thomas Hewitt, one of the promoters, invited his friend, George Newnes the publisher, to stay with him, hoping to interest him in the scheme. Newnes was a local resident and amongst other things, became a keen advocate of the Lynton and Barnstaple Railway. Newnes apparently did not need much persuasion, as he immediately came up with the money to build the cliff railway. Newnes enquired whether there was anyone local capable of building the line and was told about Bob Jones, the builder.

By 1890, the railway was complete and ready for operation. There was a ceremonial opening on Easter Monday, 1890, performed by Mrs Jeune, the Lady of the Manor of Lynton. The line was not built without opposition, for some local residents feared it would mar the beauty of the wooded hillside, for which reason it suffered a constriction that taxed the ingenuity of its designer, George Marks. Much rock cutting had to be done to maintain an even gradient. Bob Jones' grandson, also Bob Jones, said, 'The hauling was done on the upper section by using just a tin bath and a horse with a snatch-block at the top. On the lower section, they dumped the spoil over the sea wall.'

To satisfy local critics, the cutting width was so restricted that the two lines are for the most part only a few inches apart. Only in the middle section do they widen out sufficiently to allow the two cars to pass each other safely. Time has allowed the trees to arch over the site of the line so thoroughly that it is virtually invisible. The gauge is the unusual one of 3ft. 9 ins. The rails are bolted into galvanised rolled steel joists set into the concrete, the whole making a rigid construction. The total length of the track is 862 feet, with the top of the line 500 feet above the bottom. Bob recalled:

'As a kiddie of eight I used to slide down the centre rails on a bit of greased board, when they were working on repairs. The trick was to put your Wellington boot on the top of the rails and use it as a brake ... An enormous amount of trouble that passing-place cost us! The curve produced a differ-

The Lynton – Lynmouth Cliff Railway opened on Easter Monday 1890.

ential effect and, with fixed axles, you get wear on the road wheels, and twisted axles – none of which would have occurred had they allowed the railway tracks to be another 2ft. 6ins. apart.'

Operation

The novel feature about this railway, which never fails to fascinate and often mystify passengers, is that its motive power is gravity. It has no engines of any kind, only brakes. The simplicity of operation is responsible for the fact that, in its 120-odd years of life so far, there has never been an accident and seldom any serious mechanical breakdown.

Basically, it works like a pair of scales; the two cars, each of which can carry 40 passengers, are joined together on what is effectively an endless belt. Clearly, if the one at the top is loaded with more or heavier passengers than the one at the bottom, it will go down without assistance and pull the lighter one to the top. 'In that case, the passengers have worked their own passage,' remarked Bob. If, as often happens, the lower car is the more heavily laden, then water ballast comes into play. Each car 'sits' on a wedge-shaped tank capable of holding 700 gallons of water (about 2½ tons in weight), which is topped up from a reservoir every time the car arrives at the top. The reservoir is fed by a pipe from the West Lyn River and an Act of Parliament gives perpetual right to abstract water for this purpose.

When the cars are loaded and ready to move, the two drivers signal to each other by an electric bell. The brakes are then released and, if nothing happens (because the lower car is too heavy), the lower driver opens a valve with his foot and discharges water ballast until the car begins to move; this starts the top one automatically on its downward path. Both cars have governors fitted to control the speed so that the journey takes two-and-a-half to three minutes, i.e., at 5-6 miles per hour. The governors also operate a hydraulic slipper-brake, applied to the crown of the rail. In addition, the drivers have hand brakes, worked by a wheel, which grip the two sides of the rail at 1200 lbs per square inch; and these are used to bring the cars smoothly to rest at the termini. Thus there is plenty of allowance should any emergency arise at any stage of the journey.

The present water tanks are the third set to be used. The earlier ones were smaller and riveted together. Now the tanks are of welded construction, heavily galvanised and their capacity is such that the line would still operate even if the top car was empty of passengers and the bottom one full.

The design of the cars has altered over the years, a feature being that they are removable, so that freight (as was the original idea) can be carried whenever required. For safety reasons, an open platform at the rear has been dispensed with but one at the front end is for the use of the driver. Some of the wood used in the construction of the cabins came from the old Ilfracombe pier, when it was superseded by a concrete structure. Bob adds:

'Most of it is pitch pine, but there's also a bit of Lynton church in there; also some fine teak from an Elder and Fyffe banana boat that sank off the Welsh coast in the last war. Part of the wreckage floated ashore and the timber was bought from the Receiver of Wrecks.'

The two cars are joined by twin cables, 26mm in diameter, which pass over pulley wheels at the top of the incline. Two further cables are joined to the lower sides of the cars and pass over pulleys in a tension slide at the bottom, forming 'tail ropes' and completing what is in effect an endless belt. The tail ropes exert a steadying influence and are an additional safety factor. The cables have a ten-year working life, the top one being taken out to do a stint as a tail rope, replacing one which is discarded. At the bottom of each track is a hydraulic buffer to cushion the car as it comes to rest. This buffer was the invention of Bob Jones, senior, the original engineer, who patented it; but he let the patent lapse, whereupon it was adopted by railways everywhere and developed all over the world. Buffers of this type are often seen at main-line termini.

Service

As the operation of the line depends on water, frost is the greatest bugbear. The temperature now determines this and if it drops below freezing, the line does not run. The normal service is from mid-February to mid-November. There have been very few breakdowns and only minor interruptions in the service. The longest occurred in August 1967, when an axle broke and every-thing had to stop for three days. No replacement was available, so:

'We worked all night to get the broken one out and then rushed it to Barnsta-ple to have a replacement made. The new one was delivered at 7 o'clock one evening; so we worked all through that night and were ready for customers at 8 o'clock next morning'.

Nowadays, all axles are made off site by a machine shop and spares are kept on site at all times.

Besides the thousands of tourists who patronise the railway, there is a steady demand from local people who use it to go to and from work. In the early days of motoring, when many cars could not climb the steep road to Lynton, they were carried up for 7s. 6d. (37.5p) each and this has happened at infrequent intervals since. In the 1952 flood disaster, cars stranded in Lynmouth because of the damaged roads were hauled to safety and in 1970, when the road was being re-surfaced, a service was operated temporarily to save the long road journey round.

There have been three royal visits to the railway: in 1952, when HRH Prince Philip the Duke of Edinburgh visited Lynmouth after the flood; 2002, when he visited again on the fiftieth anniversary and 2006, when HRH the Princess Royal visited.

The Lynton-Lynmouth Cliff Railway is the only one of the lines round Exmoor to have operated continuously since opening. It carries around 400,000 passengers a year and since 1890 it is estimated to have travelled the equivalent of about twelve times round the earth without incident: a proud record indeed.

(I am most grateful to Ashley Clarke, Engineer and Manager, for his generous assistance with this chapter.)

Comberow
Incline.
Pontypool
loco at foot.
(H.H. Hole)

W.S.M.R. 0-6-0 Saddle tank 'Pontypool'.

Watchet – Brendon Hill

The building and operation of this line and the history of the mines it served have been related in detail by Roger Sellick in two books, *The West Somerset Mineral Railway and the story of the Brendon Hill Iron Mines* (David and Charles, 1962, 1970) and *The Old Mineral Line* (Exmoor Press new ed. 2012); and by M.H. Jones in *The Brendon Hills Iron Mines and the West Somerset Mineral Railway* (Lightmore Press, 2011). Any account here must of necessity be based upon these works, to which full acknowledgement must be given. The W.S.M.R., derelict and long deserted, provides even today a fascinating field of exploration for any wanderer among the woods and valleys on either side of the ridge that runs between Ralegh's Cross and Heath Poult Cross.

History

Leaving aside all consideration of medieval and earlier workings, it is known that by 1839 mining was in progress on the Lethbridge estate at Chargot Wood, Goosemoor and Withiel Hill, i.e. at scattered sites west of Ralegh's Cross, and that operations continued during the 1840s. By 1852, various ironmasters were seriously interested in the area and in the following year the Brendon Hills Iron Ore Company was formed by a syndicate from Ebbw Vale, which soon obtained mining rights over the territory as a whole. The company recruited labour locally and from Wales and opened an office in Watchet, the nearest port for shipment of ore.

Hitherto, all carriage had been by horse and cart but ore was piling up at different adits and shaft-heads and the need for a railway had become pressing. The company, therefore, promoted a Bill, duly passed as the West Somerset Mineral Railway Act in July 1855 and engaged Rice Hopkins as engineer. The line was to run from Watchet harbour *via* Roadwater, up to the top of Brendon Hill and then west as far as Heath Poult Cross, a total distance of over 13 miles, with a short branch east from Brendon Hill to Ralegh's Cross, where a mine was already being exploited. The track would be standard gauge, not broad, despite the prevalence of the latter in neighbouring lines.

Work began on the first section, between Watchet and Roadwater, on 29 May 1856 and was ready to carry passengers and goods by April 1857. Platforms had been put up at Watchet, Washford and Roadwater, to which point the ore still had to be carted down from the mines. At Watchet, there was still much to be done. Supposedly the responsibility of the Lord of the Manor, the harbour had been neglected for years and silting had so reduced its efficiency that vessels found it almost impossible to come alongside the pier. In view of the volume of traffic anticipated through the port, when the mineral railway came into full operation, something had to be done at once. The company, therefore, tried to make terms with the manorial lawyers but on failing to do so, promoted a Bill for the improvement of the harbour and its proper administration. An enquiry followed late in 1856, which revealed that the Lord of the Manor had no rights at all and that the harbour was public property. Eventually, a compromise was reached to allow the passage and enactment of the Watchet Harbour Bill in 1857 and for its regulation thereafter by harbour commissioners. Later, important improvements were made. The existing (west) pier was rebuilt with a jetty for iron ore and used by the W.S.M.R., while a new (east) pier was constructed which, aided by the facilities provided by the West Somerset Railway (later absorbed by the G.W.R.), catered for general cargoes. As related elsewhere, proposals were made about this time to link the W.S.M.R. and the W.S.R., generally to expand outlets for the iron ore trade and particularly to push a line through to Minehead as an alternative port to Watchet; but the plan died.

By the end of 1857, the line had been extended from Roadwater to Comberow, at the foot of Brendon Hill, and work was proceeding with the station buildings and other equipment still required for the section completed to

Brendon Hill, the remains of the winding House. (Tim Edmonds)

Gapworthy Station in 1983. (Tim Edmonds)

date. But the major task lay ahead; the construction of the incline, about ¾-mile long up Brendon Hill at a gradient of 1 in 4; to be ascended and descended by ore wagons controlled by winding gear installed in an engine house at the top. Progress was slow but the need so pressing that the incline was already in use by the end of May 1858, motive power being supplied by a stationary steam engine and so continued for nearly two years. The winding house was ready by March 1859 but another year elapsed before the iron drums were in place. The transport and erection of these 18ft. monsters must have been a prodigious undertaking and it is a salutary experience to stand at the head of the incline today and try to visualise how the job was done.

By now the worst was over. Watchet was operating adequately as a port, the railway had been built all the way from the sea to the top of Brendon Hill, where numerous lines were being laid out to individual mines. The network

Rails of the W.S.M.R. on Watchet's West Quay. (Tim Edmonds)

was basically longitudinal: at the eastern end the Ralegh's Cross and Colton group; in the centre the Burrow Farm mine; at the west and principal end all the mines round Luxborough Road, Goosemoor and Gupworthy, where the line ended. No extension was ever built to Heath Poult Cross or beyond towards the Eisen Hill mines in the Quarme valley, because the prospects of workable ore soon petered out.

Service

As the railway was primarily industrial, no official opening took place but on occasions passengers, other than miners, were carried and in 1864 plans were prepared to run a regular service from Watchet to Comberow as from the following year. Before this could happen, the line had to be passed by the Board of Trade and a good many improvements had to be completed as a result of the inspector's report. Finally, the line was formally opened on 1 September 1865, with appropriate celebrations. A service of four trains each way was worked up, each 'leg' taking forty minutes. The time was cut by ten minutes during the last eleven years of its life, viz. 1887-1898. Passengers were allowed to travel up the inclines at their own risk and as far as the terminus at Gupworthy.

The success of the railway depended entirely on the profitability of the mines and although it is difficult today to believe that the number of passengers rose from 13,000 in 1866 to 19,000 in 1872, it must be remembered that at the height of prosperity in the 1860s and 1870s, there were some 750 people in the mining community in addition to the farm folk around. Prosperity, however, did not last long. It lasted as long as it did thanks to the introduction of the Bessemer steel-making process, which made full use of the Brendon spathic ore, production exceeding 40,000 tons a year, 1874-1878. By this time, however, cheaper Spanish ore was capturing the market and prices fell so alarmingly that all the Brendon mines were suddenly shut down in May 1879. Production was re-started after a few months but the end was now in sight. Final closure took place in 1882-1883, followed by sales of equipment, land and buildings.

The railway did not close. Astonishingly, it survived another fifteen years and although many of the mines sidings were removed, the incline remained open and the section to Gupworthy, albeit deteriorating fast. The service was soon reduced to two trains a day each way. In 1891, the Board of Trade ordered the W.S.M.R. to adopt the block system, but relented when application was made to work the line on the 'one engine in steam' principle. Other requirements, such as the fitting of vacuum brakes and the interlocking of points and signals, were simply overlooked for the time being. But it was this, and the virtual run-down of the whole system, that led to its closure at last on 7 November 1898. Most of the engines and rolling stock were taken back to Ebbw Vale, the rest were broken up. There was a coda to this sad story in that, on 28/29 December 1900, a violent storm caused serious damage to Watchet harbour. Since the harbour commissioners, who owed their origin to the W.S.M.R., were unable to raise sufficient capital for repairs, their powers were transferred to the newly-formed Urban District Council, which finally restored the port in 1904. And this had another unexpected outcome.

The Somerset Mineral Syndicate

The engineer in charge of the harbour rebuilding, H. Blomfield Smith, generated such an interest in the Brendon mines and the W.S.M.R. that he formed a syndicate in 1907 to re-activate both enterprises. He bought a Metropolitan District Railway engine and a mixed collection of trucks and started repairing the track. On 4 July, amid enormous local enthusiasm, a train of sorts ran to Comberow and back and a few days later the incline was again in use. Mining was concentrated on the Colton workings, east of Ralegh's Cross, and on a new tunnel at Timwood, close to Comberow. A 2ft-gauge light railway was built from the head of the incline, past Ralegh's Cross inn, to the head of another incline, where winding gear hauled trucks up from the Colton mine in Galloping Bottom, 250 feet below. At Timwood an adit was driven 1600 feet into the hill in the hope of striking ore veins already tapped higher up. Neither of these two ventures yielded profitable results. A desperate bid to process and sell the soft ore by erecting a kiln and manufacturing briquettes also came to nothing. The railway relapsed and the whole undertaking had to be wound up in 1910. Once more the equipment was dispersed by sale and engine and wagons transferred to the G.W.R.

It was not, however, quite the end of the W.S.M.R. In 1911-1912, an Australian company leased a section of the line between Watchet and Washford to demonstrate a new method of automatic train control. The Angus system, as it was called, depended on electrical contact between a shoe on the locomotive and a ramp between the rails. This gave visual indication to the driver in the cab and, if necessary, applied the brakes automatically; a system very similar to the one developed some five years earlier by the G.W.R. Two G.W.R. tender engines were used for the demonstration, which took place on 5 July 1912 and for the purpose of this exercise, a temporary connection was made between the W.S.M.R and the G.W.R. lines. A.L. Wedlake of Watchet remembered the occasion well. It was an excellent excuse for local celebrations, a marquee was erected and the hillside by Kentsford served as a splendid natural grandstand. Most people, Mr Wedlake said, were secretly hoping that the experiment would fail with spectacular results and that the apparatus would not prevent the two locomotives from crashing into each other head-on. Alas, the trials were an unqualified success and were followed by further experiments before 1914.

The W.S.M.R. metals survived until 1917, when they were commandeered for munitions and removed by a local contractor, who started at the Gupworthy end and worked his way back to Watchet. The great winding drums were blown up. For a short time, a narrow gauge line was relaid between Watchet and Washford for the carriage of timber to Washford sawmills, mules pulling the wagons but this was the very last time the line was used. Meanwhile, some lively litigation was being conducted between the Ebbw Vale company and the W.S.M.R., which still received rent for the track and which, by spending a minimum of money on the permanent way and the buildings, kept open the possibility of re-use. In the end, it accepted a compromise sum and agreed to abandonment, which was formally authorised by private Act of Parliament on 2 August 1923. The final sale took place a year later.

Engines and rolling stock

The W.S.M.R. began with two 0-4-0 saddle tanks by Neilson of Glasgow, known, for reasons of shape, as 'boxes'. They spent most of their working lives on the upper section of the line, on top of Brendon Hill. Occasionally, when engine power was short below the incline, one had to be lowered gently on the cable and since they were liable to foul the cable guides, the latter had to be removed and replaced after the operation was over. One of these engines was returned to South Wales when traffic fell away after the mines closed; the other lasted until the turn of the century. In 1857, two 0-6-0 tanks were ordered from Sharp, Stewart & Co. to work the lower section between Watchet and Comberow. It seems that only one actually arrived and was called *Rowcliffe* after the secretary of the company. The sister engine was to be named *Brendon* but there is no record of its delivery. For some years, *Rowcliffe* coped with all the traffic on the lower section but it was eventually returned to Ebbw Vale when the mines first closed. When the passenger service started, another engine was ordered from Sharp, Stewart & Co., transported on a broad gauge well-wagon to Watchet Station and named *Pontypool*. It survived the crisis of 1883 and, apart from occasional absences for overhaul, worked the passenger line alone until final closure.

The 1907 venture introduced the Metropolitan District Railway 4-4-0 side tank locomotive No. 37, a Beyer, Peacock engine, with a copper-capped chimney. The metal numbers on the chimney were soon removed, as also the condensing gear fitted to engines which had to avoid excessive steam when working on the London Underground. This was sold to the G.W.R. in 1910 and finished its life in South Wales. Of passing interest were the two small 0-4-0 side-tank engines that worked the 2ft.-gauge line to the Colton mines, one by Bagnall, the other by Kerr, Stuart, both bought second-hand.

The W.S.M.R. carriages, all three (or four) of them, were primitive four-wheeled affairs. First and second class compartments were upholstered, third class were 'hard-sitters'. Lighting was by oil lamps. The goods wagons were likewise of a very simple type, mostly with dumb buffers, though latterly some had spring buffers at one end. The 1907 syndicate purchased 15 steel-sided tip wagons, properly painted and identified; also some wooden trucks, probably bought from the Birmingham corporation reservoir at Elan Valley.

Route

Today, quite a lot of evidence remains for the careful explorer: two lengths of track set into the surface fabric on the west pier of Watchet harbour and vestiges of the original station buildings in a garage and some private flats. The track bed is traceable alongside the W.S.R. line all the way to Washford, where it turns to pass under the A.39 and continues past Cleeve Abbey to Torre (the site of a siding), Clitsome and Roadwater, hugging and crossing the Washford River through pleasant meadows. Roadwater was once a substantial station (now a bungalow), with a platform, outbuildings and sidings. Thereafter, the line has been incorporated in the by-road to Pitt Farm and Comberow, the official terminus, where passengers used to transfer to an open truck, fitted with plank seats, and take their chance for the rest of the journey. In fact, though several accidents happened on the W.S.M.R., only one occurred on the incline (in 1882) and that was not fatal.

Today, the setting around Comberow is less obviously dramatic than it was, because thick undergrowth and trees have concealed most of the incline. Yet, after ninety years or so of abandonment and the erosion of rushing streams, the bed is remarkably intact, while the culverts and retaining walls remain a tribute to the workmanship of the past. On the top of Brendon Hill, at first glance, there is not much to see: a few hillocks of spoil long overgrown, and the scattered ruins of mine buildings and cottages, south of the ridge road. But persistent enquiry will lead you to many of the adits, now sealed or fenced and along the old track to the ghost terminus of Gupworthy. Perhaps the most striking reminder of a short but ruthless past is Beulah chapel, still in regular use. Gupworthy chapel was demolished in 1976 and has been replaced by a bungalow. However, the miners' 'dry' and stables are just still standing, although roofless. The remains of the winding house are also to be seen. From there, you can look upon a magnificent landscape of woods and valleys all around you and far north towards the coast of Wales, whence came the enterprise for this abortive Somerset Rhondda.

Today

Much research and excavation of a limited number of mine sites was conducted by the Exmoor Mines Research Group (now disbanded) over the 1980s and 1990s. With considerable co-operation of various land owners and Exmoor National Park Authority, a successful lottery bid was secured in 2006, enabling certain conservation works and purchase of the incline, now listed as a Heritage Monument. At the closure of the project, a small group of volunteers formed the West Somerset Mineral Line Association.

The Association promotes the history of the mineral line by conducting regular guided walks, conservation of the site where possible for future generations, information sheets and newsletters. Members have secured a limited number of artefacts and exhibit these items at venues in West Somerset, notably in the Watchet town museum, on an annual basis.

For further information visit www.wsmla.org.uk

(I am grateful for the assistance of Phil Gannon with this chapter.)

Junction of the track-beds near Brinsworthy Bridge: to Florence Mine (foreground). Heasley Mill (right), and North Molton (background). (Colin Thornton)

South Molton – Heasley Mill

South Molton is fortunate in having a borough museum full of fascinating items of local history, ranging from ancient documents, pewter ware, weights and measures, farm implements, fire engines and, of particular interest, the Rottenbury collection of mineral samples from the mines of the Mole valley, centred upon North Molton and Heasley Mill, a few miles to the north of the town. After this, you will be unable to resist exploring on your own. We are obliged to J.M. Slader and John Rottenbury for much of the information that follows.

History

The mines are to be found in four main groups: the *Florence* mine and its associate adits lie about one mile to the east of Heasley Mill, under the lee of Tabor Hill. Tradition says that the mine was first worked by German miners brought over in the sixteenth century; but the main period of development took place during 1870-1890, when a large quantity of spathic iron ore was extracted, suitable for steel-making by the Bessemer process. Sporadic attempts were made during the twentieth century to start the mine again: in 1918 with the aid of German prisoners-of-war; in 1942 by a group of Canadian army engineers, who barely escaped disaster due to flooding and in 1949, when a private application was refused by the planning authority on the grounds of amenity.

The *Bampfylde* or *Poltimore* mines are located at Heasley Mill, north of the Methodist chapel, beside the road to Fyldon. The gaunt stack of the engine house and other extensive ruins and spoil, tell the story, supplemented by three big shaft-holes athwart the Mole valley. Copper was mainly mined here, some iron ore and a very little gold (mostly in the iron), though a nugget was reported to have been found at the *Poltimore* in 1852. All these mines were worked spasmodically in the seventeenth and eighteenth centuries and are mentioned in the local histories of Polwhele and Lysons; but the main period of activity coincided with that at *Florence,* in the last half of the nineteenth century.

The *Britannia* mine is in the general area of Higher Mines Wood, about 1000 yards south-west of North Radworthy, close to Barham Bridge. Gold was struck here in very small quantities in 1815 but the main product was copper extracted in association with the *Bampfylde*. The *Crowbarn* (or *Croborn*) mine, located in Crowbarn Wood, south-east of Heasley, was exploited for iron ore during this same period. All mining activity, other than attempts at reopening, had come to an end by about 1900.

Route of the railway

Before the 1870s, all mineral ore extracted was conveyed by horse and cart or packhorse along the roads and tracks to the main towns and ports. This must have limited the output of the mines, no less than the dependence on water wheels and horse whims for pumping out the shafts. The introduction of steam engines for pumping necessitated a more efficient means of transport, provided in 1874 by the construction of a narrow gauge tramway, which linked with the main line about half-a-mile east of South Molton Station, reached by the D. & S.R. the year before. The point of the junction is in the fields below East Marsh Farm and although broken in many places, the banking is still visible. Further on, the line by-passed North Molton (a typical mining settlement with many reminders of its industrial past) to the east and continued to Brinsworthy Bridge, where the embankment is still visible. At this point, the track divides and the junction can be seen on the ground, with the original line travelling north-east to the *Florence* mine, and the branch north-west to *Crowbarn*, where the stables for the horses that pulled the trams were sited. The line stopped short of Heasley, as all the copper from those mines was transported by cart and packhorse. It is possible that steam locomotives were used on the section from South Molton to *Florence* or *Brinsworthy*.

A proposal to extend the line and convert it to regular passenger use was put forward at one time by the borough of South Molton, with stations at North

Molton, Heasley Mill, Yarde Gate and Challacombe, after which the line would have followed the contours to around Parracombe and thence to Lynton. This extension was by way of alternative to the Bray valley project but in the end nothing came of either scheme.

The miners

In *The Exmoor Review 1969*, John Rottenbury wrote:

'Many miners took advantage of the line to ride down the valley to North Molton, where they passed their leisure in the numerous pubs. The return journey in the up-going wagons would get them back to the mine sufficiently recovered for the next shift. Much has been written about the bad working conditions, with the miners portrayed as little more than slaves. In fact, the majority were contractors, known as 'Tributers', and mined the ore much as independent contractors in farming and the timber trade operate now.'

South Molton must have had its share of troubled times too. In the museum there is a fearsome display of wooden truncheons which, the caption proclaims, were issued to the local constabulary to quell the riots in 1830. However, it seems that they were not used to quell any riots as such but principally to deal with the miners who descended on the town on Saturday evenings, when the place was transformed into something resembling a Wild West frontier town. At a time when some 200 men, many of them from Ireland, Cornwall and Wales, were employed at the *Florence* mine alone, the scenes can be imagined, although it may seem hard to believe when one walks through the quiet town today.

In an article in *The Exmoor Review* 1979, M.H. Jones gives a very full account of a wartime effort to revive mining in this area. As a result of the U-boat blockade, a drive to increase home production of iron ore was essential. Home ore department engineers looked afresh at the history of Exmoor mineral operations. For various reasons, fully explained in the article, two sites only were considered as worthy of further investigation. The first at Blackland mine, near Withypool, was soon discarded, both because of the variable quality of the ore and because of the meagre deposits that remained. The second site was the *Florence* mine, where initial samples suggested the presence of a reasonable quality and quantity of ore *in situ*. However, repeated flooding created such problems that operations had eventually to be abandoned and so peace returned to the area.

1015 Minehead to Bishops Lydeard train arriving at Watchet in August 1987, headed by 2-6-2T No. 5572, on loan from the Great Western Society at Didcot Railway Centre. (Robin Madge)

PROJECTED LINES
Two Valley Projects

Projects for railways that never materialised have been outlined in the introduction. All occurred before the end of the nineteenth century and two are
described in some detail in the chapters that now follow. Mention, however,
must first be made of two others that merit more than a passing reference.

The Barle Valley Railway

This proposal was dated 1877. The 2-foot gauge line would have started near
Marsh Bridge, just north of Dulverton, and then run along the east bank of the
River Barle, terminating at Lower Cleeve Field, Withypool. The purpose was
to link up with the Pennycombe Water group of mines (Blackland-Halsgrove)
for the transport of iron ore. Length of line: about 9 miles. Two Dulverton men
were named in the prospectus: engineer Miles and county solicitor Samuel
Hayman Warren, besides Parliamentary agent Manning at Westminster. One
wonders why the line did not start at Dulverton Station (about 2 miles south of
the town at Brushford) and obviate the need to cart the ore from the terminus
at Marsh Bridge to the railway at Brushford. The answer probably lies in the
fact that the promoters were hoping that the recently constructed Devon and
Somerset Railway (later taken over by the G.W.R.) would itself fill the gap, and
that the iron ore trade would encourage the D. & S.R. to build the branch to
Dulverton which, in any event, was being contemplated. It never materialised
nor did the Barle Valley Railway. Had the link been made, transhipment would
still have been necessary from the trucks on the narrow gauge to those on the
broad gauge line, a costly and tedious business. Later, it was planned to transfer
the ore from the mines by aerial ropeway from Picked Stones to Porlock Weir
but that, too, remained a dream.

The Bray Valley Railway

Backed by local landowners and authorised in 1885, the route proposed ran
from Filleigh Station (on the D. & S.D.R.), northwards *via* Proutworthy Brake,
Kimbland Cross, Mockham Down Gate, Ridge Gate, Friendship Farm (then an
inn), ending short of Blackmoor Gate at the turning to Wistlandpound. One
copy of the plan and schedule is in the possession of Bratton Fleming parish
council. The engineer was C.H. Meyer. A year later, powers were obtained to
extend the line to Lynton and in 1887, to build a branch down to Combe Martin;
but no part of the route ever took shape.

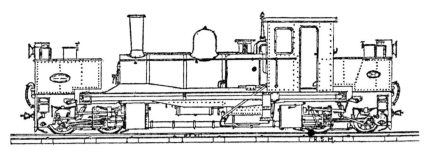

A suitable type. 0-4-4-0 Garratt No 1. Tasmanian Railway.

Minehead – Lynmouth

For the following brief account of a line which, though it had distinct poten-
tialities as a scenic route, was barely ever an economic possibility, we are
indebted to the late Jack Hurley, former editor of *The West Somerset Free Press*.
In his article '*The railway that never was*' and in contemporary reports of the
scheme, will be found all the material for this chapter.

History

Following the success of the Lynton-Barnstaple line, plans were put forward
in 1898 to construct a new railway linking Minehead, Porlock and Lynmouth.
This, too, was to be narrow gauge (1ft. 11½ins.), on the grounds that it cost
less than standard gauge to build in hilly country, despite the fact that the
actual costs of the Lynton-Barnstaple line had been twice as much as the
original estimate and that the builder had run into financial problems. On
the other hand, narrow gauge construction had proved popular in North
Wales and the Welsh connection was emphasised by the fact that two
companies, the Barry and the Vale of Glamorgan Railways, were behind the
new scheme.

At bottom lay the hope of developing Minehead as a maritime resort, with a
new pier and improved harbourage facilities, accommodating steamers
plying to and from Bristol and the Welsh coast and bringing large numbers
of visitors to explore and enjoy Exmoor scenery. The ordinary commercial
carrying trade, for coal, lime, cattle, *etc*, was also used as a line of argument
but it was not expected to compare with the possibilities of tourism.

Local opinion was divided. Prominent among supporters was George Fownes Luttrell of Dunster Castle, whose family had earlier taken the initiative in extending the main line from Watchet to Minehead and who was personally promoting plans for Minehead pier. He was backed up, generally speaking, by most of the local authorities, who wanted better communications, and by a mixed bag of persons who were able to see something in the new scheme of benefit to themselves. They included hotel and shop keepers and a number of farmers and traders, one of whom promised 700 tons of goods a year, while another spoke of sending, in season, 25 tons of whortleberries a day to Minehead. The rector of Culbone, who clearly had no fears of recrimination from his congregation, was in favour; and so, surprisingly, was Arthur Heal, the renowned huntsman of the Devon and Somerset Staghounds, who argued that the line would stop deer running to the cliffs or into the sea; but he was almost alone in his contention. The great majority of hunting people claimed that the line would separate the culverts in Culbone woods, 'where the deer lay up' from the open moor and would otherwise damage the hunt overall. Sir George Newnes, chief promoter of the Lynton-Barnstaple line, feared competition, though precisely why it is difficult to see, whereas it is easy to understand the objections of the licensee of the Anchor Hotel at Porlock Weir, since he kept a livery stable to supply transport between Porlock and Minehead.

The main opposition, however, came from land owners over whose property the line would run and from others who sought to preserve the amenities: on which grounds all kinds of people (including some Royal Academicians, who could hardly have known much about it) were induced to sign a petition against the project. Tourism was disliked because, it was argued, the line would attract large numbers of day trippers, regarded as very vulgar and objectionable people, who were likely to lower the tone of northern Exmoor, and whose cash would not offset the trouble they brought. At the public enquiry at Minehead on 9 August 1898, George Luttrell and his friends argued forcefully in favour of the proposals. They denied that the scenery would come to any harm and pointed out that that the roads were too few and too poor even for local requirements. Snow often stopped all traffic in winter and even in good weather coaches took four hours to cover the twenty miles between Minehead and Lynmouth at a cost of 6s. 6d. for a single ticket, 8s. 6d. return and 11s. 6d. if you came back on a later day: whereas the railway would offer return fares at 10s, (first class), 6s. 8d. (second class) and 3s. 4d.

(third class). None of these arguments sufficed, however, to convince the Commissioners who, knowing that the land owners would not sell, refused to sanction compulsory powers. And the story ended there.

Route

At the enquiry, the engineer designate, Sir Joseph Szlumper, also responsible for the Lynton-Barnstaple line, outlined the route that the railway would take. At Lynmouth it would start at The Tors on the high ground to the east, turn north towards Countisbury common and proceed behind Kipscombe to County Gate, and thereafter along the coastal fringe (north of the present A.39 road) *via* Yenworthy, Broomstreet and Yearnor, through the woods on a falling gradient down to Porlock. From there, it was to continue along Porlock vale, between Selworthy Beacon on the one side and the heights of Horner on the other, more or less following the main road as far as the outskirts of Minehead, where it would swing east round the town to link up with the G.W.R. terminus. At this point it was also planned to build a line along the front to Minehead pier. In the event, the pier proved the only part of the scheme to be implemented, built in 1901 and removed in 1940 since it restricted the field of fire of the coastal defences in the event of an enemy invasion.

There is no doubt that between Porlock and Lynmouth the line would have afforded passengers views of surpassing grandeur: across Porlock Bay to Bossington and Hurlstone Point, and on clear days over the water to Wales. Between Porlock and Minehead the scenery would have been less startling, though of much beauty. Yet it is hard to believe that the line would have done any better than the Lynton-Barnstaple, for the circumstances were similar. Local goods and passengers would have been insufficient to carry the annual cost and the line would have foundered before the saturation of the roads had generated a genuine demand for railway revival.

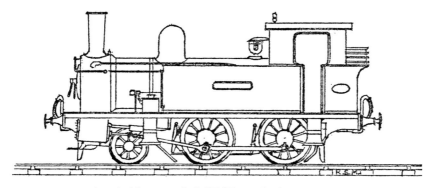

A suitable type. 2-4-0T 'Tenterden' K. & E.S.R.

Simonsbath – Porlock Weir

The story of this line, known officially as the Exmoor and Porlock Railway, is entirely associated with the exploitation of the Simonsbath estate by John and Frederic Knight in the ninteenth century. The classic account is contained in *The Reclamation of Exmoor Forest* by C.S. Orwin, as revised by R.J. Sellick (David and Charles, 1970). This is the principal source of information; other sources include *The Exmoor Mineral Railway* by G.L. Gettins (*Exmoor Review, 1967)*, S.H.Burton's *Exmoor* (Hale, 1984) and Sellick's article *A Railway 'Ghost' on Exmoor* published in the November 1986 issue of the *Journal* of the Railway and Canal Historical Society.

History – The great reclamation

In 1819-1821, John Knight, an ironmaster from Worcestershire, purchased the greater part of the former Royal Forest of Exmoor, an open waste, once a hunting ground reserved for the king, then leased to a warden for extensive grazing, and finally enclosed by Act of Parliament in 1815. By the time John Knight had completed his purchases from the crown and adjoining land owners, large and small, he had got together over 15,000 acres, almost all of it hill and moorland, with one homestead at Simonsbath. It was here that he proceeded over the next twenty years to plough, sub-soil and drain large acreages for arable cropping; raise beef, sheep and horses; plant hedges and trees; build roads and farmsteads; create a village at Simonsbath and, as a result of his labours, cause to emerge a parish and community of over 300

Here the track crosses the Porlock-Exford road at OS 845451. (Arthur Phillips)

people on Exmoor. His son, Frederic, took over in 1841 and continued to administer and develop the estate until his own death in 1897, when the property passed to the Fortescues at Castle Hill.

Mining

John Knight was an industrialist and both he and his son were venturers in the best sense. It was their desire to develop all the resources of the land, below as well as above ground. Mining, particularly, was in their blood and John Knight had made sure of acquiring the mineral rights when he bought the land. During his lifetime, however (he died in 1850), very little prospecting had been done. In 1846, a local syndicate secured a lease to exploit a site known as Wheal Eliza, on the River Barle below Simonsbath, for copper; but though work continued intermittently for nearly ten years, little copper of any value was found. However, the mine yielded promising quantities of iron ore and it was this that decided Frederic Knight to buy back the lease in 1855 and re-assign it to another party. But the iron proved a disappointment too and by early 1857, all work here had come to a stop.

Meanwhile, Frederic, fired by the success of the mines in the Brendon Hills, organised trial diggings in other parts of his estate and invited expert opinion. He was led to believe that he was sitting on a vast reserve of iron ore, mainly around Cornham, Burcombe and Hangley Cleeve and he continued to believe it long past the time when all attempts at mining had had to be given up. For a few years, however, the prospects seemed excellent and in December 1855, he signed a lease with the Dowlais Iron Company on the basis of £1000 a year 'dead' rent plus a royalty of 1s. per ton of iron ore raised. Moreover, in 1856 and 1857 he signed leases with two other syndicates for the exploitation of sites elsewhere on the estate. All these undertakings, however, failed. Although the quality of the ore was good, the quantity was insufficient and by the middle of 1858, all exploitation had ceased. This, too, was the end of serious attempts at mining on the Simonsbath estate, though the lure of Exmoor iron was such that a second series of enterprises was launched shortly before the First World War but they, too, failed.

The railway

One of the Dowlais principals was G.T. Clark, a railway engineer by profession, who had worked under Brunel and gained experience of railway construction in India. It was partly due to a personal visit by him to Exmoor that the Dowlais company prepared, from the first, to play a positive part in solving the problem of transport. Together, Clark and Frederic Knight worked out on the ground a possible route for a railway from Simonsbath to the coast, where both Lynmouth and Porlock offered possibilities as ore ports. In the end they decided on Porlock Weir, where Colonel Blathwayt, the local land owner, was building a dock. It was further decided that whereas the Knight estate would build the railway, Dowlais would supply all the rails and ironwork and both parties signed a separate agreement to that effect in December 1855.

Frederic Knight pressed ahead at once, negotiated with Colonel Blathwayt and in January 1859 applied to Dowlais for the delivery of the rails. Meanwhile, as related, all mining activities had ceased and, following a court judgement late in 1859, the company paid over a large sum of money in order to terminate its lease. Frederic Knight maintained, however, that the railway contract, being an independent agreement, was still in force, whereas Dowlais contended that their part in furnishing the rails and other materials was conditional upon setting the cost against royalties for the mined ore; and that since there was no ore, they were automatically released from the second contract. To force their hand, or so it seemed, Frederic Knight signed a lease with Colonel Blathwayt in 1860, on the understanding that he would build the line within five years, and on 4 December let out the construction of the track in lots to local contractors by public auction. Dowlais sent agents to watch proceedings both then and later and soon formed an opinion that Frederic Knight was not in earnest. The company was right. Very little work was ever done, most of it confined to surface clearance of the ground between Whit Stones (at the junction of the Exford-Porlock road) and Warren Farm, and ultimately the matter was concluded by a further payment in 1862 and the handing over of all mining works, buildings and equipment to the Simonsbath estate.

Frederic Knight made one further attempt to salve the enterprise by forming an independent company to construct and operate the railway. Nothing, however, had matured by 1865 when the Blathwayt lease ran out.

Route

At Porlock Weir the line would have run westward along the shore as far as Worthy and then travelled up the steep by two inclines (with a level section half way up to Yeanor Mill Bridge) to the coastal road at the top, 1400 feet above the sea. In this first section, the motive power would have been assisted by gravity, descending trucks laden with ore pulling up the empties, as in the Brendon Hills. Thereafter, the track was relatively level for 6½ miles between Whit Stones and Warren Farm, following a winding course, crossing and re-crossing the Exford road at two points and keeping to the high ground in the general area between Larkbarrow and Alderman's Barrow, round Swap Hill, Elsworthy and Ware Ball. G.L. Gettins describes it as follows:

'For most of its length it consists of two parallel low banks about 18ins. high and 27 feet apart at the top with a flat 'road space' between. It is often obscured by heather and rushes, but clearly identifiable when seen lengthwise. The banks seems (sic) to be spoil heaps of surface peat and soil cleared from the road space. The bank on the uphill side is usually the larger, and may have served to deflect surface water to culverts at intervals. It does not seem sufficiently wide or of suitable material to carry a railed track, which, presumably, was to have been laid on ballast deposited on the road space.'

From Warren Farm one can only guess at the final section of the route. But there is later evidence to suggest it would have continued along the 1400-foot contour towards Exe Head, crossing the infant River Exe by a bridge west of Blackpits and then circled south towards Prayway Head, where either it would have descended by easy stages *via* Dure Down to Cornham Ford, or dropped by a third incline to a point close to Simonsbath, with extensions to the mines.

The line would have been nearly 14 miles in length, of standard gauge and, apart from the inclines, the trucks would have been pulled, possibly by ponies, more likely by locomotives (limited to a speed of 12-15 mph) of a type illustrated at the head of this chapter.

It is of some interest to record that when mining was resumed, 1910-1914, the ore was transported by steam traction engines, running over roads constructed in the first instance by John Knight.

An earlier plan

A letter at Somerset County Record Office makes it clear that John Knight had had an idea for a railway at a much earlier date. In this letter, dated 28 November 1826, he asked Charles Bailey, agent to the Blathwayt estate, for a lease of land 25 feet in width for the purpose of a 'Rail Road, with inclined planes from Porlock to Exmoor Forest', with additional space at Porlock Weir for wharves and buildings and the power to divert streams for various purposes including, possibly, the operation by water power of the inclined planes. This letter was never answered, despite a reminder dated 23 June 1827, but had the proposal been accepted, the problem of haulage might have been solved at the Porlock end, with one interesting variation. The line would have run direct from the Weir to Birchanger, where the Blathwayt estate ended, and then *via* Hawkcombe (not Whit Stones) into Knight property. What about the descent into Simonsbath from Prayway Head? The 1855 scheme envisaged the use of a stationary steam engine and tends to dismiss the theory that John Knight had constructed Pinkery pond and its canal in the early 1830s for water power to operate the incline. In any event, in 1826, the iron ore deposits were undiscovered, although John had purchased the mineral rights when he first acquired the Royal Forest. Orwin thought that the pond had been intended to provide irrigation water for the long stretch of land from Pinkery Farm to Honeymead and Sellick agrees with the suggestion by Roger A. Burton (*Exmoor Review* 1984, p.71) that the railroad was intended to bring lime to the acid soil of Exmoor.

Select Bibliography

G.A. Brown, J.D.C. Prideaux, H.G. Ratcliffe: *The Lynton and Barnstaple Railway.* David and Charles, 1980.

S.H. Burton: *Exmoor.* Robert Hale, 1984.

C.R. Clinker and C. van den Arend: *The West Somerset Railway.* Exmoor Press, 1986.

Ian Coleby: *The Minehead Branch 1848-1971.* Lightmoor Press, 2006.

Freddie Huxtable: *The Taunton to Barnstaple Line.* Lightmoor Press, 2016.

M.H. Jones: *The Brendon Hills Iron Mines and the West Somerset Mineral Railway.* Lightmoor Press, 2011.

Richard Jones: *West Somerset Railway – A View from the Past.* Ian Allan, 1998.

Chris Leigh: *Portrait of the Lynton and Barnstaple Railway.* Ian Allan, 1983.

Robin Madge: *Somerset Railways.* Dovecote Press, 1984.

Colin G. Maggs: *The Minehead Branch and the West Somerset Railway.* Oakwood Press, 2011.

Colin G Maggs: *The Taunton to Barnstaple Line.* Oakwood Press, 1980.

Colin G. Maggs: *The Barnstaple and Ilfracombe Railway.* Oakwood Press, 1978.

Vic Mitchell and Keith Smith: *Branch Line to Minehead.* Middleton Press, 1996.

C.S. Orwin and R.J. Sellick: *The Reclamation of Exmoor Forest.* David and Charles, 1970.

John Parsons: *Saving the West Somerset Railway – The Branch that refused to die.* History Press, 2011.

R.J. Sellick: *The Old Mineral Line, Watchet to Brendon Hill.* Exmoor Press, new ed. 2012.

R.J. Sellick (and others): *The West Somerset Mineral Railway and the Story of the Brendon Hills Iron Mines.* David and Charles, 1970.

J.M. Slader: *Days of Renown.* West Country Publications, 1965.

Allan Stanistreet: *Portrait of the West Somerset Railway – 25 Years of Preservation Progress.* Ian Allan, 1996.

David St. John Thomas: *A Regional History of the Railways of Great Britain. Vol. 1 – The West Country.* David and Charles, 1988.

A.L. Wedlake: *A History of Watchet.* Exmoor Press, 1973.

A.L. Wedlake: *Old Watchet, Williton and Around.* Exmoor Press, 1984.

Lyd *entering Woody Bay* (Keith Vingoe)

Isaac *at Woody Bay – high summer.* (Keith Vingoe)

The Authors

Robin Madge

The late Robin Madge was Head of the Art Department at Huish's Grammar School in Taunton, now the Richard Huish College, for twenty-two years. Though born in the Wirral, visits to relatives in Somerset made sure of his love of the county and its railways and it was inevitable that he should settle there. He passed on his love of the G.W.R. to many boys at the school and to his own son who has provided the engine drawings in this book.

A member of the Great Western Society and a 3mm Society railway modeller, he was involved in helping with the organisation of celebrations to mark the 1000th anniversary of the Port of Watchet in 1988.

Allan Stanistreet

Allan Stanistreet, like Robin Madge, originally hailed from Merseyside and in retirement has settled in Somerset, after over forty years spent in the army and the civil service. His interest in railways goes back a long way and he has been connected with the West Somerset Railway, both as a shareholder and a member of the West Somerset Railway Association, since 1974. He is still an active volunteer on the line and has six books to his credit, as well as numerous magazine articles.